BEAUTIFUL
LIKE A MAYFLY

BEAUTIFUL
LIKE A MAYFLY

by

Walt Franklin

Wood Thrush Books

Published by: Wood Thrush Books
                 85 Aldis Street
                 St. Albans, Vermont 05478

ISBN 978-0-9903343-2-3

Acknowledgements

Thanks go out to the following individuals whose assistance in one capacity or another provided me the fuel and energy to bring this book to the finish line:

Family members Brent, Alyssa and Leighanne Franklin, plus my mother, Ilse Franklin, for the light she shed on our old country roots.

Doctor George Chruney, the Music Man, laid out the sound track for my wanderings and writing efforts. Rex Marino inquired when the next book with his name in the "Acknowledgements" would appear. My friends Walt McLaughlin, Tim Didas, and Bob Stanton have stood nearby and offered their encouragement.

Scott Cornett, a fisheries biologist with the New York State Department of Environmental Conservation, lent a big hand to my stream remediation work and to my vision as a fly fisherman.

Alan Littell, a travel writer and historian at Alfred University, gave perspective and new impetus for the essay "Bright Antiquity." Sean Phelan gave invaluable feedback to the final chapter of the book. And last, but not least, my friend, Carol Bebe Wimock, unsuspectingly assisted with construction of several essays in this story of a long and strangely wonderful life.

Table Of Contents

BEAUTIFUL
LIKE A MAYFLY

Forward: Looking Back

"You're beautiful, like a May fly"
– Ernest Hemingway

I was 60 years old when I decided to pull together some loose ends of a lifetime and present a memoir. At first I was reluctant to call the work a memoir because, aside from the faddish production of this genre today, the memoir is traditionally associated with an end-of-life recollection of events before senility occurs. At 60 I wasn't feeling terminal as yet, but I was no longer stunned when fellow workers asked me about retirement or when my kids joked about my age. A time arrived when this book just wanted to be told. The book wanted to present itself with a "double focus," as Canadian writer Tony Cosier put it when describing one of my earlier works. In addition to being a personal narrative, *Beautiful Like a Mayfly* was to be a natural history of my encounters in society and in the wild. Recalling poet Robert Bly's notion of "two-fold consciousness" (a state of being that's informed by a blend of personal history and "universal news"), I aspired to that sense of layered consciousness, and hoped my readers would discover it too.

Turning 60 might have seemed a shade formidable, but it was nonetheless like witnessing a landmark. The story of one life was ending as another tale began. From here I could look back at personal origins and put them in the framework of my "three-score years and ten." I saw myself at age 24 moving into a rented house with Lisette Bodian in the deeply wooded Fall Creek valley, a home only 10 miles from the place where I'd eventually settle and spend the greatest portion of this life. Fall Creek was a turning point in my development, a place I've written about in early poems and in the book *A Rivertop Journal*. Fall Creek was also a springboard for my upcoming years in northern Virginia, reflected in "Old Dominion," the first essay of this book, and for an exploratory period spent in Europe and remembered in such essays as "First Spring, Germany" and "Bright Antiquity."

"I'm a miserable failure by any standard that's deemed American," wrote a friend of mine who's a good published writer with a less than typical inclination for commercial success. I realized I, too, was a failure in that regard, having even less aptitude for an income than my writer friend, but that was okay. Long ago, in my Fall Creek period, I took a half-hearted stab at being a "failure" in the eyes of the American standard. I knew I'd love to sell books eventually, but living an honest, healthy, and full life had to be a top consideration. As the poet Lew Welch said, "Look, if nobody tried to live this way, all the work of the world would be in vain." This voice, this sentiment, was one the poet hoped to pass along to the sons and daughters of America. Welch suggested that every once in a while a son or a daughter got the message. In *Ring of Bone*, he said, "Now and then a son, a daughter/ gets away."

In my view, I was a lucky one, a kid who got away into the Fall Creek woods. I never learned how to make much money, but I found a way to live. With the creek or the river as a metaphor for life, I would soon be wading against the current. To wade in such a manner would become a theme for the days and years to come. If civilization had a wicked flow at times, this was the best way I could serve it.

These, then, are my tales of stepping through the waters, enjoying the pools and riffles, and occasionally getting swept downstream a ways. In any case, I've tried to keep my senses open and, even while standing still, have tried to keep on the move.

– Walt Franklin, 2014

Old Dominion

1

It was one of the coldest winters on record for the Shenandoah River Valley. On the evening of February 2, the temperature plummeted again. My wood supply was wet and I had trouble keeping the stove sufficiently fueled. Gripped by winter ennui at the age of 28, I didn't feel that my work, either as a residential teacher or as a writer, contributed much of a spark to anyone's regeneration.

Stepping out at 7 p.m., I looked for the star Aldebaran positioned in the head of Taurus the Bull. The science world had predicted its occlusion, a temporary, shadowed disappearance. I couldn't find it, so retreated from the cold, but an hour later it was there—the heaven's thirteenth brightest star, 64 light years distant. Inexplicably, I looked to it as a beacon.

On another night I was reading "Devotions" by the poet John Donne. Poetry warmed the bones of winter, and I flashed on a memory from youth. When I read, "Thou hast imprinted a pulse in our soul, but we do not examine it; a voice in our conscience, but we do not hearken unto it," I remembered skipping school one day and walking through a field near home. In the green seclusion of the moment I stumbled on a red fox stalking prey. I was close to the hunter, transfixed. There seemed to be an orchestration of events going on that would include my winter thoughts so many years later. I read some words; a memory surfaced and then disappeared; it was no stranger than Aldebaran playing in the shadows of space. There was nothing religious about it; I just figured that a human's night receptors were more active than our daytime senses. And yet I knew that a wheel was turning and that nature was communing after dark.

Early one morning the thermometer registered minus 16 degrees Fahrenheit, frigid by Virginia standards. To look at the sun reflecting from the patterns of frost and snow was breathtaking. While holding an axe in readiness for chopping wood, I saw a Carolina wren dipping in and out of spaces made by stacks of oak and locust wood, looking for the ease of summer insects locked inside the loosened bark. I swung the axe to warm myself, and soon noticed that the temperature was climbing. By midday the thermometer read a balmy 22 degrees, a rise of 38 in just four hours. A one-eyed cardinal, a male, joined the ranks of other songbirds at the feeder.

After another night of zero degrees I found that our inefficient woodstove couldn't thaw the creaking and arthritic bones of our old cottage. The water pipes had frozen. I got them loosened up eventually. They cleared with a last convulsive spit of slush. Relieved, I took a morning walk to the nearby Shenandoah. Ice and snow covered three-quarters of the river surface. Dark water wove a jagged course through the whiteness. With a blue sky overhead the scene was deceptively tranquil, like a view I once had from the window of a jet plane heading westward over Labrador, waterways looping through a frozen wilderness that rose imperceptibly from the sea. The river's surface made me think of Walden Pond, as well. Thoreau's readership generally disregards Henry's sense of humor, but I thought of how he once suggested using a divining rod to locate water while he stood on top of Walden's ice and snow—an example of "dry humor" at its best.

At home I watched the dark-eyed juncos hopping over the crusted and unbroken snow, over the bright yard with its shadows cast by trees, where I had scattered seeds to eat. The tree shadows looked like open channels in the river ice, the whole yard like the bare bones of a stripped-down season. Trout, the shepherd-collie dog, rambled through the yard, approaching me on the porch, without disturbing any of the birds that fed just feet away from him. I often frightened the same birds with a mere motion at the window.

One day after catering to the needs of flu-infested students, I returned home feeling ill and listless. Snow was falling heavily. When I woke next morning, even the serenity of a new 18-inch coverlet of snow failed to stimulate me till I'd built the wood fire and consumed huge quantities of hot herbal tea. Improved, I walked out into a record-breaking whiteness. I waded freely down an unplowed driveway to the mailbox. The air was windless and the sky was clear. The land was yet unscarred by human initiative. I looked to the fresh tracks of my inquisitive dog and then to a red-bellied woodpecker circling the snow-free surface of an apple tree.

A man shoveled his driveway to the river road. The grating sound had a muffled tone that faded into airy silence. When a plow arrived at my own place I was reconnected to the town. Left with less simplicity and understanding than I had before the road was opened, at least I was feeling good, my health restored. *The Washington Post* had called the storm "the worst in 50 years." While complaining villagers dug their way out of it, I enjoyed the fact that traffic had been snarled, that airports had been closed, and that commercialism had been stalled. "Bad ass weather," grumbled Pappy, our school custodian. I heard no grumbling from the students, and imagined Henry D. Thoreau reiterating, "There was never yet such a storm but it was Aeolian music to a healthy and innocent ear."

I accidently left my wallet on a vending machine in the local laundromat. I had filled it with dollars after cashing a paycheck. I was in a grocery store when I realized what had happened. I rushed back to the laundromat, expecting the worst. An old woman there had picked it up. She returned it to me with the full amount enclosed, chiding me for leaving the wallet where any one of the village's "coloreds" could've taken it, leather, license, lucre, all. She was an honest person but prejudiced, proving again that honesty and love don't necessarily dwell in holy matrimony.

By the third week in February I found that a walk along the creek behind the cottage was the medicine I needed. I stepped through the deep snow and the brown rangy bodies of last year's teasel plants. Domestic pigs lounged indifferently on the banks, the wildness of their boar antiquity frozen like a fleck of ice in their brains. Beyond them were several tufts of rabbit fur and a streak of excrement on the snow, followed by

15

the print of owl wings telling a tale beside the sycamores where a cardinal was bursting into song.

As the temperature climbed into the fifties, the male song sparrows added their sonorous notes to the air. With the breaking of weather came the rupture of a bathroom pipe that left me with a pond before I could leap stocking-footed toward the cellar to close the intake. The gush of water rang its theme of damage and expense, but a damned fool standing cold on his sopping feet could only think of spring.

The plumbing of society had another twist in its ruptured belly, a crisis with familiar groan, a warning of what was to be. The Western World was re-experiencing a "gas shortage," and its mobility was affronted. We listened to the options put forth by our energy czars but didn't hear much about reducing our dependence on fossil fuels. Crisis was one thing and addiction was another, and the two were intertwined. And if we needed a distraction from the crisis, we could look to the appearance of digital screens and to computers. Modern opiates could ease the daily grind, like teachers and policemen rallying school kids to deplore the use of drugs. We would all get by.

Following a two-day rain with melting snow, the Shenandoah River overflowed its banks. Water backed its way up a feeder stream and flooded the road. A man's car was stranded in deep water where our driveway joined the river road. The man had driven foolishly on the inundated course until stopped by surging water. I saw the old guy and his poodle trekking up the lane. "Mister, I'm in trouble!" he exclaimed, his pants and shoes wet, the tweed jacket and the hat still dry. He was shaking and becoming incoherent. I ran for the landlord's truck but couldn't start it. I made a call, and soon a tractor from the monastery, a mile away, rumbled into the swirling flood. I waded through the icy water to my knees and helped attach a chain, then entered the stranded Ford and steered it while a great machine pulled me onto drier ground.

It was the day and the hour of a solar eclipse. The only light from the damp and somber afternoon seemed to issue from silver rain beads strung like tiny lanterns from each twig of bush and tree. The winter star Aldebaran had been shadowed for an hour back in February, but the only occultation I could sense now with the eclipse was that of the river road beneath a flooding Shenandoah. Then, as evening fell, the sky began to clear, and warmth entered the valley like a flock of red-winged blackbirds from an arc of joy.

2

The valley thrummed with new life. Along the creek I watched a pair of bluebirds perched in the full light of a dead tree. Silver warbling blended into background calls of grackles, mockingbirds, and cardinals. Three broad-winged hawks soared northward on migration. At home, chipmunks scampered in the yard and roosters crowed. I played new music by the likes of Eno and Cluster on the stereo, the crystalline melodies sounding spacious, and the odd rhythms complementing an emergent season out-of-doors.

As the Voyager spacecraft passed the planet Jupiter, an editorial in *The Washington Post* suggested that we humans had failed with our inner searching and our spiritual quests; we needed to renew collective excitements and discoveries by supporting travel in space. Sitting on the porch, I looked up from the newspaper and saw the source of a shadow gliding across the yard. A vulture drifted downhill over the treetops, the only spaceship my imagination needed at the moment.

Trout, the dog, was napping on the driveway when he heard a chainsaw start up at the neighbor's house. He rose and padded down the drive as if with important business to investigate. At the junction of the driveways he turned toward the main farmhouse, looking for the source of the commotion. I decided to check the mailbox. Inside it was an advertisement dropped off by an emissary from some church, declaring, "Be not deceived... Awake! The end of all things is at hand." The message stated that, of all humanity, only the chosen few would be saved. Damn it, I thought, and just when things were starting to look good for me... and thus I wished for a dog's life that had only chainsaws for concern.

I waded to a leafy island in the Shenandoah. Paired mallards and wood ducks drifted on the shimmering channels, and a pileated woodpecker flew overhead. This island near the monastery was close to a half mile in length. At its north end I could see a second island out beyond the main river channel. During the Civil War these islands and adjacent fields had played a role in the Battle of Cool Springs, but today in the solitude of Sunday afternoon they were new lands entirely. I was like Columbus in my waywardness, like Robinson Crusoe in imagination.

Home again, I reminded myself that I'd been living along a feeder stream for almost three years now and couldn't remember the name of it. Checking a wall map, I read, "Wheat Spring Branch." As with any place where I was spending time, I wanted to map the territory in my head and understand its position in the realm of life, but I was working slowly. No problem. The various locales surrendered their secrets at whatever pace you wanted to discover them—to learn of their histories and tales and interdependencies.

So I paused on a bank of the Wheat Spring Branch, looking at the rolling pastures, an Arcadian landscape with a creek flowing through it, nibbling at the soil and sycamore roots and wine-colored bushes. I worked on a map for my head. That night, the evening of the Equinox, Bebe and I celebrated with friends at the bar on Mt. Weather. Later, at home, with the spring's arrival at 12:22 a.m., I continued the fun by tossing Trout a grilled cheese sandwich while absorbing some cheap Portuguese wine. The sky was full of stars, and the creek babbled from its run. We howled to the heights above and drove the owls to puzzled silence.

Fortunately the songs of spring were prettier than our human noises. With the final thawing of the winter muck, they rose from the drainage ditches and the wood duck haunts, a tranquil piping and a perfect antidote to the blues. From the wet cornfields by the river to the Appalachian Trail that lay on the mountaintop, I heard peepers and wood frogs and varieties of birds ushering in the flowers like hepatica and bloodroot. Fresh sights and sounds converged in a rush of blood that felt like freedom.

If I was free by American standards I was also relatively poor. Being "free" was worth the cost. I could work my limitations to advantage by admitting I had freedom of movement. As the late Beat-era poet Lew Welch put it, I could "move with leisurely grace, alert so as not to get run down." When a money-grubbing or consumerist society faced me in the ring like a Spanish bull, I could step aside and watch the "huge machinery" roll by, not really seeing me at all. It was a youthful dream that I continued to live with through my twenties. The direction of it was uncertain but the willingness to submit to nature's way was sure.

One night I stepped to the proverbial side with a group of off-duty teachers and counselors from my school. With a full moon glowing above the bar on Mt. Weather, we were witnesses to Bob M., the owner, cranking up the jukebox for the song called "Take This Job and Shove It." Bob had been listening all night to snippets of conversation otherwise alien to his regular blue-collar customers: chatter about pragmatism vs. idealism, of popular music vs. alternative rock, of world philosophy vs. trivia from the life at Grafton School. The old man looked on paternally and took our dollars, scratching his round head. When Bob closed the curtains at 1 a.m., the 10 surviving patrons howled dementedly from his parking lot and triggered a menacing response from his coonhounds penned up in the backyard of the tavern.

Driving home, Bebe and I found a great horned owl standing on the river road. Its marble eyes glinted fiercely in the headlights as we stepped from the car and watched the facial disk so focused upon our approach. The owl's head shifted for the possibility of other dangers. We wondered if the bird was wounded or possibly stunned by an auto. Bebe wanted desperately to help the creature but we watched it make a short, clumsy flight into the grass, clicking with a sound like two stones struck together. I felt the good vibes from the earlier hours fold up into a resignation to fate.

20

Next morning I searched the riverbank but the owl was nowhere to be seen. Had it found a place known only to dying owls, or had it survived by simply hopping from this dangerous alleyway of human life to fly again? With luck, it was free of restraints, free in life or free in death, the greased machinery having missed it after all.

3

I took my vision of the big owl to the woods. Again my purpose wasn't clear, but as Black Elk, the Native American tribal leader, once said about visions, it was the quality that matters; it was the intensity of the emotional response that drew one forward. So I drove with the spirit of an owl beside me from the river valley to a Blue Ridge mountain where a gravel road grew narrower and the forest on each side reached inward toward the car as if reclaiming something lost or stolen. When the remnant farms came into view, I parked.

The owl spirit seemed to beckon where the toads and hylas had recently piped their mating calls. Armed with old binoculars I entered a realm of sweet and musty odors, of quieting birds, a brook flowing under sassafras. A Carolina chickadee approached me on the road and I thought of Bebe's comparison of a chickadee to a "maître d' with a top hat and a bow-tie."

Even in the owl-light before dark, I could tell that the foliage was at its peak, the leaves still young and fresh, unscathed from the heat and insect hunger soon to come. A June bug skittered through a redbud tree; a last ovenbird sounded with a *teach!* cry.

As if from a glow in the western sky, I heard the rasping note of an American woodcock announcing the occasion of his nuptial flight from an old field into the space above. Typically the male bird starts at a bare spot on dampish ground and ascends with diminishing spirals to a point 200 feet or more above the field. Climbing, he pulls the air through primary feathers, which produces a distinct twittering sound. Descent is a zigzag motion from which the woodcock spills a tumbler of warbled chips. All the while, the bird's intent is to reassert his woodcock territory and impress a female of the species. The flights are an event I look forward to each spring.

The *peent*, or the nasal-sounding call note of the woodcock, resembles the first utterance of a whip-poor-will, another species I looked forward to encountering. A whip-poor-will flew in from the distance like a sudden breeze laden with the scent of garlic (a plant common on the mountain). It settled on a fallen branch adjacent to a split-rail fence festooned with honeysuckle. The male gave its call-note then proceeded with the famous song, which rang out clear and tremulous, plangent and repetitive. The song was sounded at a speed of 50 to 60 calls per minute and in runs of several minutes at a time. It was the proclamation of springtime in the Blue Ridge. There was much to see and hear.

More whip-poor-wills flew in and settled near the caller. A trio of the birds called out intermittently with a chilling vibrato pitch. I caught a glimpse of white tail-feathers in flight, reminding me of daylight slipping into darkness. I felt safe there on the mountain and returned slowly to the car. Then something split the night and brought me to a stop.

A pair of light beams shot across the mountainside and a two-note chopping sound of motors dominated the environment. The lights pierced the darkness overhead and a locomotive roar deafened my position near the car. For a moment I had no idea what was going on, but as the great disturbance lessened and the night's tranquility returned, I remembered I was poised on the wooded carapace of a city designed for Armageddon. A pair of military helicopters had forged on to the "Installation" at Mt. Weather, a short distance up the slope.

Inside the wire borders of the heavily guarded Installation there's a way to drop down to the belly of the beast inside this mountain. That's where more than two thousand federal guns, along with families and selected V.I.P.s could circulate among sophisticated war rooms, stores, and living quarters carved out from the rock. That's where the elite would ostensibly survive if and when the world as we knew it dissipated in flash and smoke. It was 1979, and I was as close as I'd ever come to this subterranean suburb of modern city life, and I felt sure that at least one waiting Soviet missile had a number for the ground beneath my feet.

Somewhere down below this stomping ground for woodcock and for whip-poor-will there were simulated battles played out daily in the minds and on the screens of people who knew nothing of the rural lives that gathered for a beer and a song at Bob's tavern or of wild birds that had flown here for millennia. I heard a humming sound that seemed to ooze skyward, nailing down my nerves and muscles for another moment before the darkness and silence of the mountain were regained.

Driving home, I crossed the river with my windows down. Hundreds, maybe thousands, of amphibians rang their mating cry to the mountain air, and I imagined the magnificent cacophony eventually mingling with the songs of woodcock, whip-poor-will, and bob-white, even with the songs that wafted out of tavern doors and opened windows of speeding cars. That joyful noise from the interface of the animal and human realms marked the *real* power of the planet, or so it seemed. If nothing else, one human had the power to believe it so. The cosmos had the ultimate authority, of course, a power to wipe clean the slate of human dynasties in time. It was comforting to think that the earth and the sun and even the star Aldebaran would always have a say in matters, but the notion wasn't quite enough.

Still restless, I reopened *The Anatomy of Melancholy*, an ancient tome by the historian Robert Burton. It was good to review an underlined passage there that said, "Life is governed by chance, not wisdom" – seven words to sleep on in the shadows of Mt. Weather.

First Spring, Germany

1

The great twin spires of Cologne's cathedral rose above the double arches of a new McDonald's. Riding the train in a roundabout journey to my grandmother's home near Nuremburg, we passed forsythia and magnolia blossoms floating in the factory smoke of late April. We passed sporadic views of castle ruins on a steep cliff of the Rhine, of walls and towers, vineries, gardens, strolling lovers, pheasants, and billboards announcing yet another place of famous breweries. A drunken Italian directed us to happy lodging near the city of Strasbourg, France. The walls of this old college town were splashed with revolutionary slogans. The cathedral with its single spire was an imposing sight: a renowned rose window on the burnt exterior, plus flying buttresses, gargoyles, dark interior with angels wrestling on the pillars, and a wonderful celestial clock. The intricate timepiece is replete with cogs and gears, Apollo and Diana, Death with his bell and scepter dicing up all existence. And yet, as Bebe and I stood beside the great clock of the cathedral in 1979, I had no way of knowing that in more than 30 years into the future, I would have a daughter spending a semester in this city, who would have a view of this cathedral from a window in the home where she was staying. Bebe and I enjoyed two fine trips to Europe, but within a year of our stop in Strasbourg, we would go our separate ways.

We hit Interlaken, Switzerland on the holiday known as May Day. Men and women wore traditional Bavarian clothes and traveled with hiking shoes and skis. Bad weather had befallen the tourist town but I was glad that we were here in May rather than August. Rain and snow seemed easier to deal with than a horde of tourists.

The name Interlaken means "between the lakes." Founded in the thirteenth century, Interlaken still retains an old city gate, a quaint landmark in a town of high-rise structures. Surrounding us were many lakes and ponds, chalets and pasture walkways, and snow-capped mountains. Brown Swiss cattle foraged in the dandelion meadows; and people strolled the *wanderweg* or rode their bicycles on inter-village trails, reminding me that here the Europeans were more involved with outdoor life than Americans were in much of my homeland.

Snowfall in the higher country kept our prospects limited to the valley. One morning we awoke to see the sun reflecting beautifully from several mountains named Jungfrau, Monch and Eiger, all about twelve-thousand feet in altitude. We took a walk on one slope where I tried to apprehend the spirit of its place by looking for birds. Earlier, the dawn chorus of birds had been a jubilant affair in the alpine dimness, and now I recognized a few of the songbirds—the European blackbird, closely related to the American robin, singing from the roof peaks, chimney tops and cherry trees; the jackdaw, a sociable little crow that flies around the eaves of houses or soars above the village; and the song thrush living up to its name by issuing a variety of flute-like notes. I recognized the jackdaw as the probable species evoked by Pieter Brueghel, the Elder, a favorite painter artist, in his "Winter Hunt," from times when I studied a print of that remarkable painting. Dandelions seemed to push up through the fresh blanket of snow. Inside the forest, we passed small shelters and benches placed for walkers, feeding stalls for deer, and houses for the birds. A white wagtail appeared beside a mountain creek and then we saw our first European dipper, a dark stub-tailed bird with a large white throat-patch. The bird flew above the swiftly flowing stream then lit upon a rock, bobbing once or twice before submerging to the gravelly bottom. Birds were emissaries for me, capable of reporting in their way about the old-world charm and beauty found beneath the surfaces of things. As we left the high peaks region en route to Zurich, we departed with regrets, not knowing if we'd see this kind of splendor again.

I had passed through Zurich six years earlier and remembered my passage there as strange but intriguing. It had been the home of Carl Jung, the great doctor of the deep unconscious mind, and of Tristan Tzara, the writer and the so-called father of surrealism. My memory of Zurich was connected somehow to the vagrants, boozers, prostitutes, and tourists I ran into in the old, bustling city. On this occasion, Zurich didn't offer us anything but a passage on to Liechtenstein, a

27

tiny mountain nation found between Switzerland and Austria.

Six years before I'd done a winter hike on a mountain rising from behind the prince's castle near Vaduz, Liechtenstein, but now we passed through the little kingdom too late in the day to do anything other than backtrack to Sargans, Switzerland. When morning found us in Sargans, we climbed to a castle high on a grassy ridge. The castle's gray rectangular walls seemed to lift out of vineyards rife with birdsong. We overlooked a valley of woods and meadows where the clang of cattle punctuated a fresh medieval charm. New homes could be seen a short distance from the valley floor but beyond them the mountains raised their snow hats to the sky. We would soon reenter Germany and its Black Forest region of Bavaria. There the dog-sized deer (reh), the small farms and the streams would blend in with a darker realm reminding us of Grimm's fairy tales, of witches, innocence, and blood-letting. But a wondrous view of the Sargans valley would remain with us throughout.

In Munich we toured the Jagdmuseum with its artifacts emphasizing man's emergence from the world around him, and we lingered in the Alte Pinothek, the old art museum with its famous paintings. The works by Altdorfer and by Durer were of special interest to me. Altdorfer (1480-1538) was among the first Europeans to paint a canvas without *Homo sapiens* as the primary subject. His "Donaulandschaft bei Regensburg" is a fine landscape of blues and greens with a roadway cutting through the forested hills toward a castle in the background. I appreciated the position of that castle.

Albrecht Durer's work amazed me. His "Oswald Krel" (the Green Man in Moss) seemed apropos to my recent reading of *Sir Gawain and the Green Knight*. But my favorite museum piece was Altdorfer's "The Battle of Issus," a massive masterpiece of detail, action, color, and emotion. Its foreground is a hive of human killing and destruction. Mountains in the background gently draw the viewer into a transcendent peace. Fantastic.

Bebe and I made our exit from the Renaissance world into the city mall. There the crowded techno-ambience felt almost feudal. Pedestrian. My attention shifted to a young woman walking in front of us – her tight clothes and high white boots insisting on observation. As she turned, her long hair and shadowed eyes gave way to her escort. I stopped in astonishment and then called out. The guy walking with the young German woman was Hartmut Spang, my mother's cousin who resided in Schwabach, a small city south of Nuremburg.

So Bebe and I were introduced to Ulrika who had just picked up Hartmut at the Munich airport! They invited us to ride with them to Schwabach, our ultimate destination. After a tall glass or two of wheat beer we were speeding northward on the Autobahn, listening to the latest Roxy Music album in a BMW that just as easily could've been a time machine zipping from the background of an ancient painting to the foreground of an abstract on the future.

2

Schwabach was hard for me to recognize. We were in the middle of a two-week holiday celebrating spring

(Fruhling). Bakeries and specialty shops were selling chocolate bugs as big as sunflowers. What I'd remembered of the old city's flair was lost in a blaze of carnival rides, concession stands, and American soldiers whirling around like calculations in computer games.

My grandmother had died a few months earlier. Our plan was to stay at her house until my mother arrived from New York in a week or so. We made a futile search for a family friend, Werner, who was holding the house key for us, so we took a hotel room and then visited a bierfesthaus where bored Americans sat around drinking Miller Lite and wishing they were home. A few of them tried to steal some beer mugs but were apprehended by the tent police. It was good to finally locate Werner and the house key, which allowed our entry into Oma's place.

The morning sun shone on the yard. Although a needle factory west of us belched out an occasional cloud of smoke, bees and butterflies probed the secrets of a miniature garden. A turtle dove cooed, and people clattered by on foot, strolling the pedestrian lane that led downhill toward an ancient city gate, or, heading in the opposite direction, walked down to the marketplace of Schwabach. Small daisies blossomed over moss, and peering down between the grasses and the leaves, I thought of Albrecht Durer's "Still Life."

Later I was stretched out with an excellent German beer. The lawn had yet to be mown this season. Bebe, lying on a towel beside me, was asleep; her brunette hair sprawled against the verdant grains of May. Beyond her was a walkway to an opened entrance lined with yews and roses. The rough exterior of the house was softened by an orange-yellow cast, the pallor of an age as old as America. Dark shutters lent an accent to the double stories of the steep-roofed structure.

A redstart (*Phoenicurus phoenicurus*) perched on a steel pole that extended from the roof peak of the terra-cotta shingles to the power lines. The bird fluttered off to the city wall against which my grandmother's house had been constructed. The house, situated at the outside of the city's western wall, had probably been built in some politically stable era long after Schwabach's wall had been cobbled together in the thirteenth or fourteenth century. Fragments of the wall remain in a few places around the city, and here I could see how the original must've risen from rectangular blocks of sandstone. The fragments were pockmarked with age. Small birch trees rooted in the wall and wrestled skyward, testament to the plant kingdom's tenacity and strength. We rested on a quarter-acre of antiquity and freshness, transient as a bird.

I was born in a hospital less than a mile away. This was the place of first memories. Here I'd lived until the age of four, and it was strange to think of the house as a home. But my grandmother's parents had bought it in the 1800s, a house already two centuries old at the time. By any standard of human residence, that meant it was pretty well established, and it allowed me to think of myself as native.

3

We listened to a Schumann concert, Leonard Bernstein conducting, on commercial-free television, a nice follow-up to a documentary on Germany, circa 1940-

1945. The female narrator spoke calmly about the Holocaust and of her experiences during the war. Film depicted a pastoral scene in springtime, then with bloodied bodies scattered in the grass. It displayed a lampshade made of human flesh. A woman's head was shrunken and preserved on a stick. The narrator, as a girl, had walked along a roadway, her face beaten and swollen, darkened by rape and torture. In the vast framework of the scenes were sirens and explosions, pillage and prayer, people running through the streets— nothing new to me, who recalled the stories of my mother's family during wartime, how they'd run for safety even from the house where Bebe and I were staying. Listening to Schumann helped us look ahead.

In the early mornings I could hear the blackbird chorus, the dark thrushes, songs from the neighborhood, bright notes overlapping and entering through an opened window. The chorus was joined by notes from the European robin (actually a warbler, not a thrush) and the blackcap and the blue tit, among others—birds that came to the garden and the feeders helping me to cope with the present time in relation to the dark light of recent human history. Deutschland was a country of birth—my mother was born in Germany; my father had been a U.S. Air Force gunner who stayed here to work the first years of the Occupation. I was a kid of the fifties when my father took us to America.

Hitler was a world away but still an element of the torn fabric here. Whatever wildlife I could find helped me bide the days and hours till my parents and sister came to join us at the house.

A street car shuttled us through a wooded area before discharging us at the Nuremberg Zoo. The zoo's ambience had more nature in it than other zoos I've visited. Wild birds, such as robin, song thrush, redstart, jay, and fieldfare, pecked at grains and insects in the larger cages and flew freely. I was more interested in them than the monkeys and gazelles. I felt relaxed under the uncommon hardwood trees where a red-tufted squirrel bounded across the path in front of us.

Later we toured old Nuremberg and enjoyed a modest meal of bratwurst and mustard in a hard roll, with beer. It was like a modified stadium snack in America. Curious, we stepped inside the Frauentormaur, a small red-light district tucked against the city wall a few blocks from the train station.

Red lamps glowed from each side of the narrow cobblestone street as women of all shapes and sizes and constituencies applied their ancient trade from windows and from corners, and as men, both young and old, leaned against the city wall or nonchalantly entered doorways.

Hand in hand, we thought of it as a drive-thru meat house where the motion of feet replaced the rolling of wheels. Painted eyes winked from nodding heads; sequined bras and colored panties hid the likelihood that pain and loneliness were the landlords here, that bliss and devilry were merely tenants. The red zone had its rightful place in the city but I thought its cobblestoned walks were somehow connected to cemented trails at the zoo. As we quickened our pace to the train station, I imagined ourselves more like birds that entered and exited the cages than the stranded animals within.

One night, for a change of pace, we entered a gasthaus off the market square in Schwabach. A group of young folks drank together in a small room, but we joined an older man beyond who was affable and conversational at first, but who silenced himself on learning we were *Amerikaner*. He had been a prisoner of war. After I explained that I was born here, he requested my mother's maiden name, which I gave him. He came to life again, stood up drunkenly and staggered off to ask Maria, the elderly waitress, if she'd ever heard that German name around this place. When the old soldier slumped back to our table he reported that he'd once had a friend with that unusual name, but through our ensuing breakdown of communication there was no way of knowing whether he actually knew a family member or not.

We had more luck at a second inn that night. It was filled with Greek card players. Many Greeks and Italians had come to Germany for work following World War Two, and many of them stayed. I noticed that every tune on the jukebox here was a Greek import, with exception of "Disco Baby," an obvious American classic. All but two of the card players were a somber bunch. The standouts were the tall, nervous bartender and a middle-aged fellow with dark receding hair, black-framed glasses, and a trace of mustache. The latter claimed to be broke and argued with the barman, saying he couldn't pay for the beer. The edgy bartender stepped up and began to frisk the patron till he found a bill tucked in the checkered jacket of his suit. The card players seemed disinterested in the action though we heard an occasional chuckle. Then the scowling patron, with his money found, shuffled to the jukebox where he dropped a few coins (probably for "Disco Baby") but got nothing in return.

The card players, spread across four tables, were engrossed in the game. Each card was dealt with a blurred motion of the hand. Each card was slapped down violently with a smacking sound, as if with a rapid strike from behind the player's head. Had we been card players ourselves, these fellows would've been instructive.

My relations from the U.S. came at midday, along with our German friend, Werner, who supplied us with a case of a rugged beverage known as Shaffbrau. It was good to have the family members aboard. My father hadn't been here since his work in the 1950s and he was looking forward to a hike in the Black Forest. My mother's intent was to sell the house and property as soon as possible, not that she really wanted to. This was the home where she had spent a lot of her youth. We sat around the dinner table, ate our various German foods, and felt the shears of fate begin to cut the tether.

Bebe and I reflected on a Bierfest conversation we'd had with a couple of U.S. military personnel. We'd been nibbling on white radishes and biting into pretzels the size of steering wheels when I asked a soldier how he liked the German beer. "It's bitter," he replied. I then asked him if he really meant "better." No, he retorted. "It's bitter!"

On Mother's Day the five of us visited my grandmother's grave and placed plants and flowers from her garden on the raised earth. All around us people were working as if to make the wooded cemetery look like Eden. It was a mournful hour but the songbirds trilled from the sunlit conifers above. German bodies were housed in cheap degradable caskets underground. Their plots had ten, twenty or thirty-year leases on them, to be renewed eventually, or to have another casket replace the old. In a land where open space was at a premium, this system of burial seemed reasonable, if cremation wasn't an option. For a while, the dead lived on in the hearts of their survivors.

I sat with Bebe at a fifteenth-century café by the Albrecht Durer house in Nuremberg. It was a quiet area overshadowed by the city castle on a hill. Pigeons plummeted from a blue sky; sunlight filtered down through chestnut leaves and blossoms while artists sketched and bare-chested youths drank beer and tossed their frisbees on the square. We spoke about my father who had gone on his trek to the Black Forest, decked out in a new Bavarian hat and with a rucksack. We talked about my mother's vigorous attempt to sell the house. Apparently the neighbors were interested in buying it for rental property and for turning the garden into a parking zone. "They paved paradise / And put up a parking lot," sang Bebe, quoting the singer Joni Mitchell.

Looking down at the old sidewalk I saw the hoof print of a pig. Beside it was the carved signature, "Vollendet 1273," still legible despite the flight of centuries. The sun shone everywhere, in opposition to the sense of melancholy that began to rumble deep inside me. When an overweight man, dressed in pink and brown, came waltzing past our table, skipping and laughing outrageously, I couldn't even smile. I felt like a waterspout on the St. Sebold Cathedral nearby, a demonic creature with protruding upper mouth, big ears and brows, stupid to the ways of change. I felt lousy till the mimes came by, performing with musicians on the sidewalks of the square. At the chiming of the five o'clock bells I felt improved, less of a drag on poor Bebe and, if not exactly resonant as the tintinnabulation of church bells, at least mellow and not so freighted with the sense of passing time.

4

I set out by myself one morning and paused on the small pedestrian bridge that crossed a stream known as the Schwabach River. I recalled vaguely how I played down there along the stream when German was the only language that I knew. Walking onward to the city's edge, I came to the carp pond with its chaffinch and a wagtail bobbing near the reeds. Beyond it, in the wide agricultural fields I saw a female wandering on a path and picking flowers. I thought of Wordsworth's poem "The Solitary Reaper" and felt transported briefly into nineteenth-century England. The romantic in me paused to wonder what her motivation was, what brought her here on a walk collecting flowers.

In a forest of evergreens I found a room-like clearing with sunlight spilling down, a place to recline on moss and heather and to nap with the breezes glancing off a shoulder. I was out for untold minutes till I jumped awake and startled a deer that grazed nearby.

Returning to the city I stopped for the sight and sound of a famous bird of poetry. A skylark warbled from high above the field, its song sustained as the bird circled in a way reminiscent of a woodcock's territorial flight. The lark hovered and then folded its wings for a dive back to the grasses. I wanted more, and the lark did, too.

The bird fluttered outward and ascended slowly, more directly upward than a woodcock in its climb, higher and higher as the notes poured forth. Then the skylark paused and held for a moment or two before resuming flight and almost vanishing at a point hundreds of feet above the ground. As long as I paid attention, I could hear the liquid song pouring gently from the sky. Again I stretched out on a lush green floor, just listening. With its last descent on outspread wings, I rose and left the bird behind.

A short way on, I stopped for lunch at a gasthaus. Five tables with orange plastic chairs were set up in the shade of an agricultural area. A large glass of beer tasted great. A woman came out and served potato salad, then tended her baby who was planted in an orange Mercedes carriage by the entranceway. Brown hens and crème-colored chicks paraded by the tables pecking at crumbs. Eating bread and salad, I could hear that the patrons inside were already drunk to the day. And beyond us all, the little river called the Schwabach flowed as ever.

Closer to home I had a first good observation of a fieldfare, a bluish-gray thrush with a mottled chest, attending its young ones in a short tree. Beneath the tree was a weedy ditch where, on inspection, I discovered a pair of very large snails, the size of silver dollars, copulating in what had to be the world's slowest act of erotica. I understood that whatever consenting snails did in the privacy of their molluscan realm was none of my business at all, but I became a voyeur despite myself.

One of the snails had impaled its fleshy, veined body over the other. This dominant creature with its light green body then pulled its shell up from behind, ever so slowly, into the mounting. Bodies clung, for minutes or maybe hours, to the weedy bank of the ditch.

The top snail had long tapered "horns" ending in a tiny ball. The horns wavered and then straightened. From my anthropocentric perch above the snails, it seemed as though the shells swirled around a vortex, and that the earth rattled and rolled along the meadow's edge. The climax had implications even for me. Creatures didn't need wings or opposable thumbs to make a statement through behavior. This was basic, earthbound sex, and I could see why the dominant snail dismounted even slower than it had climbed onto the other's back. The afterglow must've been disorienting.

Only an odd-duck naturalist would admit that a snail-watch was more interesting than the kind of thing you might peep at on the Frauentormauer in Nuremburg or other red-light zone. But oddly enough, I figured there was less pretension in the ditch, more energy and unspoken purpose on the weedy bank. If viewed with curiosity (for lust was not a factor), the snails could teach us a thing or two.

5

A notice for the sale of the house was entered in the local paper, and response to it was immediate, incredible. The phone started ringing at 6 a.m. and didn't stop till late afternoon. The first visitors came at 8 o'clock. I quickly mowed the lawn and got the hell out of there. Talk about a housing shortage! The impending sale kept my mother busy all day, and when I came back for a while I watched potential buyers filing in and out, and wondered who, if any one, would give a crap about such sentimental notions as family, the history of the place, or the special qualities of a garden. In a matter of days and hours, I'd be closed out of my European world.

Meanwhile Bebe and I shopped for groceries in the fish market then headed to the central fountains where we savored ice-cream cones laced with berries, whipped cream and rum. Cathedral bells rang melodically, and rain clouds built up in the western sky. The wind scattered white petals of the fruit trees in my grandmother's garden.

Late that afternoon, my mother announced to a lingering line of potential buyers that *das Haus ist schon verkauft*; she'd convinced a local craftsman, a young gold beater, to buy the place for his parents. He had been acquainted with the home; his mother had delivered eggs and farm items to my grandmother for years. Good news. The place wouldn't be converted to a parking lot; it had been a rapid sale.

My father met me at the house. He'd had a fine Bavarian tramp. Along with the others we visited a local gold beater's shop—the city is renowned for guys who can pound pure gold into paper-thin leaves—and celebrated at a local restaurant.

After our farewells to Germany, Bebe and I flew from Frankfort to New York. On the plane, we sat near a man who appeared to be fretful and edgy. I thought he smelled bad, also, till I realized the odor came from a chunk of Camembert that Bebe had purchased and inserted into the travel bag. Toward the end of our flight, I took out my field guide to the European birds and that caught the attention of our distracted neighbor. He, too, was a bird man, and he knew his subject well. In fact, he nearly resurrected the Latin language by reciting scientific names of many German species he'd become familiar with. He knew their songs, their call notes, and their variations; he knew about their populations and their distribution ranges. Our fellow traveler belonged to an ornithological society and was also a chemist working in New Mexico. He could joke about environmental pollution and nuclear terrorism, but he wasn't exactly likeable. He told us he had once synthesized THC, the active ingredient of marijuana, and found a way to blow the minds of laboratory monkeys. I probably wouldn't have found him memorable if he hadn't asked me what I thought about the skylark's song.

I thought back to the German meadow and recalled the songbird's bubbly music from the sky overhead. I thought of the English poets, Wordsworth, Shelley, and Keats. Our fellow airline traveler then related an anecdote about the president of the bird club he belonged to. The club leader had responded to a skylark's aerial display with, "That's no song! The bird's unfit to be the subject of Romantic poetry!" The world was a big place and it took all kinds to fill it up.

I pulled a new watch and chain from my pocket. My mother had given me the pewter watch as a gift before we left the old country. It had Roman numerals accented by a floral inlay. Its ticking was the sound of history. It was almost time to land.

Bright Antiquity

The Poseidon Tavern

Waiting for my plane at Kennedy Airport in New York, I was glad for the beer. There was a flight delay because the jet had lost an essential screw. The heated lounge was bad enough; there were also rumblings of doom emanating from the media outlets; and the sight of a woman walking by me in a leopard-skin hat deflated my attempt to explain the spectacle of a woodcock's mating flight to a man from Brooklyn. I had to keep things in perspective. I was going to Greece; I'd taken up Socrates' directive to "Know Thy Self"; I'd taken to heart the poet Shelley's declaration that "We are all Greeks."

I spent an hour talking to a tall, attractive Californian who carried a pet rabbit with her. We spoke about our hopes and aspirations, which included the desire to sit near each other on the plane, but Fate, so kind for discovering the missing screw, was cruel in matters of the opposite sex: she got row 45 and I had 33. She was destined for Sicily; I was going to Rome's da Vinci Airport with its machinegun-toting youths and then to Athens. At age 32, I was older and it didn't matter anyway.

After the procedure at customs I jumped on a bus that coursed along a shoreline vibrant with carnivals. It was the fourth week of April and I wasn't aware of any particular holiday. We passed a large sign at water's edge that read "Poseidon Tavern," which must've been the acme of saloons because it had no walls or human structure whatsoever, nothing but the sign, the sand, and the shimmering sea.

It was dark by the time I saw the Parthenon's silhouette on its famous hill. I found a cheap student-run hotel near the Plaka district and prepared to spend a peaceful night on a cot laid out on the roof. But first I entered a British pub and chatted with an older Dane from British Columbia. As I drank a couple of "Fix Hellas" beers, the Dane blessed my arrival, saying, "May the spirit of Hermes be your guide!"

With Hermes, god of trade and travelers, perched lightly on my shoulder, I began to explore the Plaka, old town Athens, situated on the northwest slope of the Acropolis. I imagined Hermes strolling rapidly ahead on winged sandals, the finest of guides, and walked amidst stone houses massed together and laced with narrow passageways. Groups of Germans, Greeks, and French, plus Japanese, English, and American people shifted about. Cats were everywhere. The city was alive with ethnic activities such as Greek folk dances, and the air was redolent with the scent of poppy, palm tree, thyme, and cactus.

I walked past the imposing Arch of Hadrian and various other ruins unrecognizable in the dark, past corner kiosks selling trinkets and newspapers, and then was sucked in to a plain establishment called "Bar, All

Kinds of Drinks." With a name like that, how could a connoisseur of cold beverages and urban life resist?

In addition to the Greek proprietor of the bar, there were only three other people in the place, a young woman sitting at each end of the long room, and a middle-aged woman on a stool at the center. It was a strategy designed to kill. The older woman was at my lap in a second, pawing for a drink. I decided, what the hell, one expensive drink for her wasn't going to hurt much. The barman approached me, eager for talk and, learning of my origin, pulled down an ancient wall map that was scrolled above the liquor bottles. He said, "Where we are," pointing to Greece, and then, "Amerika, where you are from." He claimed to love America and was pleased that a representative from the land where dreams come true was sitting in his bar and getting treated by one of "his girls." Unfamiliar with the dives of Athens, I made my sojourn brief and wobbled out, disappointed that I hadn't found transcendence in Poseidon's Tavern, but pleased that I had stumbled into Aphrodite's den which, good nights aside, might warrant further investigation.

Garden of Athenian Delights

Out of the thousands swarming like ants over the Acropolis, there was one colorful individual. He walked the pine-flanked pathways in a flowery shirt and red suspenders that supported chartreuse pants. White socks engorged the baggy pant legs, and he improvised wildly on a fine harmonica, reminding me of both Dionysus and Captain Beefheart. He entertained and he intimidated. Blowing into the mouth harp, the young minstrel made giant strides toward the gathering tourists, shaking his long curly hair. And people slunk away like shadows. As he sang and spoke in Greek, this man without borders picked up rocks and small boulders, feigning to toss them at the zombie world. With a rock in hand, he'd stamp his feet at passing motorbikes on the boulevard and even threatened to smash a slowly moving Cadillac. But mostly he created laughter and, no doubt, a questioning of reality.

I followed in his wake, perplexed and chuckling to myself. Who else could get away with threatening so many cosmopolitans? I watched businessmen cower and duck and laugh as they tried to escape his wild approach. He walked up to a beautiful woman and, escorting her along a sidewalk on the hill of gods, alternately spoke with her and played harmonica. It seemed that his quasi-courtship was appreciated. I realized his actions were no simple contrivance for attention. When the tourists had satisfied their curiosities and left him, when he was far from any obvious observer, he remained a portrait of joy and freedom—a modern Dionysus strolling with a bunch of picked flowers, singing to himself and the eternal stones.

While writing notes about him, I sat on the slick marble rocks overlooking northern Athens. I heard another man preaching or lecturing to a crowd below me. I thought of Socrates and moved closer to the man and his congregation until all I saw of him was his back, his long gray hair and dark coat. His voice carried from the rock he stood upon and seemed to float over the winding pathways underneath the Parthenon. His flock smiled and nodded its collective head. I wanted to understand the words, and wondered if he was prophet, lunatic, politico, or poet. Whoever he was, he'd found the right place for his message.

I visited the caverns where Orestes had taken refuge from the hounding Furies (the Eumenides), set within the flowered slopes of the Acropolis. People walked the dirt paths near the caves where a chaffinch sang incessantly and where blood-red poppies and mayweed blossomed in the fragrant air. But within the refuge of the caves I found excrement, trash, and toilet paper strewn about, a rank scenario, indeed. After all these years of so-called Progress, people still desecrated the ground. I stood briefly at a haven for the flies that hounded beauty like the Furies did.

In the Agora I watched an old shepherd approach an ice-cream vendor. He was dressed in heavy tattered clothes, his body as bent and gnarled as the crook he carried at his side. He pecked for coins in his hand to pay for the treat. The sight was as simple and timeless as any I could imagine. Then I saw another elderly peasant—a black-dressed woman with a deeply furrowed face. She placed a pan of steaming food on the seat of her bicycle and calmly ate a meal there as the modern city hummed nearby.

Next morning I rose from my rooftop bed at 6 a.m., thankful that my fellow travelers had been quiet and considerate to all. On the street below, someone was already playing a colorful hurdy-gurdy to the morning air. The loud harmonies spurred a stumbling wino to toss a few drachmas at the machine. I was struck by the city's alpha and omega characteristics, by its blend of East and West, of Classical and Byzantine culture, of the ancient and the new.

The National Gardens are near an area of classical ruins. Before me was the beautiful temple of Olympian

Zeus, which I stumbled on by accident. Sixteen golden Corinthian columns stood in the morning sun enveloped by a Mediterranean crispness. Honeybees worked the blossoms, and a comfortable breeze swept the mind clear of secondhand imagery. I invited the spirits of place to enter my abode of thoughts and to inform me of the land. Pagan mysteries had the sweet scent of blended tangerine, honey, and thyme. The joy of standing in the solitude of temple columns felt incomparable. With the caffeine of two wicked Greek coffees zipping through the bloodstream, I forced a salty tear from the eyes and then retreated to the role of photo-taking tourist. If the photos developed I could verify that it wasn't all a dream. Photos would be like the orange globules hoisted from the garden flowers by the honeybees, substantive but less than whole.

The National Gardens are an enclave where civility meets the jungle, where the visitor enters a Rousseau-like ambience replete with semi-tropical plants and zoo animals. I walked through intricate floral arrangements, through lush woodland with sunlight filtering through, where songbirds trilled and a peacock cried. I pulled a ripe fruit from an orange tree and consumed it near the Presidential Palace where costumed *Evzones* stood at guard. Their colorful kilts and stockings were, historically speaking, practical for both shepherding and driving back Mussolini's army. A blackbird sang, perhaps less melodically than its cousin the American robin, but with notes a little more intriguing and complex, or so I thought as I listened with blood and bone, as if I, too, had staked a claim to some new territory.

Mother Athens

The Agora was the intellectual, administrative and commercial center of Athens during the Golden Age. It was there that people listened to the orators, philosophers and pundits of the day to learn the latest in ideas and world events. In the center of its vast field of ruins I felt that my wits had finally shattered and blown away like seeds. Trying to plumb the depth of history here, a feeble mind approached paralysis. The unlimited possibilities caused a dizziness that sent me back to taking pictures. I sat on a ruin of the Temple of Ares and, as if with a snap of the fingers, raced back and forth in time. I imagined tracing the line of architecture from these temples to the Pentagon and the Smithsonian in Washington, D.C., and back to the Golden Age of Pericles. I saw tourists falling over each other to pose companions beside these ruins of bright antiquity. I had to move.

I took refuge in a small grove of orange and olive trees, and wondered if this was the spot where Socrates had been imprisoned for alleged corruption of youth. A large turtle crawled slowly through the grove, its shell reflecting a green map-like configuration. I figured that the turtle knew its way perfectly, and sensing that my own path led through the excavations, I returned to the open air as if to the ashes at the end of time. I peered into labyrinthine housing structures at ground level, noting the remnants of platforms, steps, walls, bridges, and streets. Like a turtle I put my nose to the canals of an underground system of waste disposal and water carriage. Something stirred inside the entrance of a tunnel.

A small pup was sitting there, twitching in the sun's embrace. The young dog rose from its haunches and turned to wobble farther inside where it joined eight or nine siblings. The pups huddled together, looking well fed but motherless, at least for now. I imagined them to be descended from the dogs of ancient Athens, slightly wild, reverting back slowly to the wolves that they once were, still safe from the modern city swarming outside of the Agora's fence. I half suggested that Hermes, my invisible escort, keep an eye out for them. Walking away, I saw the mother dog approaching. She was edging underneath the far fence of the Agora, thin and brown, and carrying refuse in her jaws. She loped to her litter and, at the entranceway, gave a gentle bark. The pups tumbled out into the light.

I stepped up to the Metroon, a sanctuary of the mother goddess, Gaia. It's an open-sided ruin with a mosaic floor consisting of subtly colored stones with a frayed design. The floor remained a beautiful artifact despite the weeds growing through its cracks and the effect of feet that trampled it daily. The adjoining Temple of Hephaestus, a Doric structure, seemed less impressive than the similar Parthenon. It was built in 450 B.C. and displayed a mixed bag of graffiti scrawled through the ages. The next building I encountered was the reconstructed Stoa. That's where I committed the terrible faux pas of walking blindly into the women's bathroom, which was not a classical latrine but a thoroughly modern WC, replete with a lady who quickly flushed and exited on the run.

I ate lunch under the awnings of an outdoor café. The souvlaki, salad, beer, and bread were complemented by the smell of orange blossoms. The recorded bouzouki music was inevitable, however, and droned its way as usual into every bite and inhalation.

I returned to the worn marble steps of the Acropolis. On each inspection of the partially reconstructed Parthenon on the summit of this hill, I was overwhelmed by majesty. Description was inadequate—noble, splendid, massive, practical, poetic. Adjectives failed this perfect though irregular structure. Humankind, imperfect as it was, had created a thing of beauty long ago that was no less beautiful, in my mind, than a fragile mayfly sailing on a river's breeze. Hell, I even saw it as evidence that lasting peace and progress could be made on this wayward planet. But tall orders aside, I knew that the building had been so well studied and described that I needn't worry about my own description for it, or worry of its implications for the world of art and politics.

A nearby hill is known as the Hill of Muses. I climbed that one, too, and sat near the summit and discovered that, again, the view of Athens down below was excellent. At my back was the second-rate monument to Philopappos, a Roman bigwig of the first century A.D. Across the fields of umber-colored flowers the tour buses came to a halt. This hill, once sacred to the Muses and their worshippers, was now sacred to the drachma-loving bureaucrats.

Rising from my thoughts I shook off the Muses, or at least I thought I did. Turning towards a rocky field between me and the parking lots, I saw an odd spectacle. Nine attractive women were dancing in spare clothes against the background of Acropolis. It could've been pure fantasy, but the young dancers in their skimpy, sky-blue tights and their golden, spike-heeled shoes were real, as far as I could tell. Identical costumes accentuated ample breasts and posteriors. The Hill of Muses was alive! These were not the Bacchae, priestesses of Dionysus, because their movements were too cultured and self-conscious. They were dancers for a film crew that was shuffling around and shouting directions. It was like a scene from a Fellini panorama. I wanted a photograph of the event but decided that the hill was multi-dimensional enough. I wouldn't know where to start looking for one.

Deflated at the bottom of the hill, I tried to escape the swarms of guided tourists by ducking into the entrance of the Byzantine "Cathedral of Athens" (650 A.D.). A sign read, "This is a holy place. Please enter properly dressed! Keep the body covered! No shorts allowed! Keep quiet!" I passed through the triple-arched Corinthian marble doors into the soft rays of an antiquated heaven. I did not remove my clothes. I thought of Mother Athens. There were no tourists here.

One night, in order to celebrate May Day in my never-ending quest for the perfect beer, I entered a bar and almost got myself in trouble. I met a young woman who was black-haired, thin, attractive, and it seemed like we were magnets whose ends weren't only opposites, but were closing together wickedly. She was French but had a mastery of English. With an interest in art, she'd come from a mountain farm and was saving for a trip to Africa. We drank, we talked, and we sensed that we both had an act to play. Somehow she reminded me of the dark manipulator, Julie, in John Fowles' book *The Magus*. I didn't want to think about what I reminded her of. Granted, we were in a bar, and as a plan unfolded for the next day or so, I sensed a Doubting Thomas sitting in the front row of my Theater of Immodesty either shaking his head in disbelief or giving me the thumbs-down treatment. But I left the bar alone at midnight reeling with a drunken confidence (one that Baudelaire, himself, would've smiled upon), thinking that our plan to travel together for a while was a good one, though, of course, reality would interfere next day. Eventually I would sit at lunch beneath the café awnings to decide my next move. A violinist came screeching through the dining tables scraping his Stradivarius, and a shoeshine boy approached and practically demanded that my shoes be cleaned. I think I came to a decision about the third time I explained to the kid that dirty shoes were fine with me. Freedom felt like a heavy weight on my chest, but one that I could deal with. Next morning I would walk for miles through a different Athens, through a gray, commercial, hustling place, but a train would save me and get this body moving from a station, getting it out where it belonged.

The Ring of Legend

The train passed northward through the semi-barren hills, through sheep fields with impressionistic poppies, past factories spewing clouds of smoke and toxin over agricultural land. Holiday celebrants stood near the tracks, drinking and waving and picking flowers. We were near the place of Eleusis and its literary tradition, but I caught no sense of young Persephone gathering wild things prior to abduction into the underworld, or of her mother Demeter, the corn goddess, sitting sadly underneath an olive tree as if her daughter had already been stolen. We passed precipitous banks of rock that led to water's edge, sometimes clinging to a mountainside without guardrails while a hungry sea beckoned with a gem's translucence. Finally we crossed the Corinth Canal, its blue water drawn through walls of rock as we entered the Peloponnesus.

It was a region whose history is unimaginably complex. I stepped out into modern Corinth that was built several miles from the ancient city state after the destructive earthquake of 1858. I traveled to the ruins of old Corinth and imagined what it might have been like speaking with Diogenes and commiserating with the cynic at his barrel (in which he lived) on the subject of "alienation." He might have straightened me out a little by sharing his "corrective vision" of the times.

I caught a bus to Nauplia and passed through the rain-filled mountains in the heart of a land named for Pelops, a character of the early Greek tales whose father served him as a snack food to the gods. Pelops was offered to the gods to see if they were, indeed, omniscient. As Henry Miller, the American author, once said of this region that includes Nauplia, Mycenae, and Argos: "Draw a ring about these places and you mark off one of the most hoary, legendary areas in Greece."

At a bar in Nauplia I drank a cold one and observed a donkey harnessed to a cart in front of the opened door. I found a youth hostel for the night then headed toward the ruins, most of which evoked a fairly recent history dating from Byzantine rule in the thirteenth century through succeeding volleys of control by the Franks, Venetians, and the Turks. I climbed the 899 steps of the acropolis to the fortifications first built in the fourth-century B.C. and then to the Palamidi, an immense labyrinth of stone, an "impregnable" fortress strengthened and enlarged by successive waves of conquerors. The view to the sea and to the town below was staggering. The water surrounding Bourtzi Islet cast a brilliant emerald and turquoise sheen that shifted minute by minute with the angle of the sun's rays. I was greeted by a mob of high school students wearing a Greek uniform with their country's colors, loud with yelling, singing, and playing tapes of popular music. One girl sang to Pink Floyd's "The Wall" in her native tongue: "We-don't-need-no-education." They left a wake of litter and the stink of urine at the clefts of rock.

I explored the maze of medieval architecture for more than an hour without determining its limits. I poked around the walls of a former prison for hard-core convicts and viewed its chambers of execution. I walked through arched tunnels and descended into a dungeon filled with unlovely water. It was good to resurface and climb down to the bay where a kestrel flew and the church bells rang. I had dinner at the water's edge while observing the sun broaden to an orange glow behind the mountains. The fish and salad, the fries with veal and seasoned sauce were excellent, even the taste of feta cheese was getting better. All of it got washed down with a bottle of that pine nectar called retsina wine.

Henry Miller described the road to Epidaurus in his book *The Colossus of Maroussi*: "I wonder how it is that no painter has ever given us the magic of this idyllic landscape. Is it too undramatic, too idyllic? It is sheer perfection, as in Mozart's music... One stops searching. One grows silent, stilled by the hush of mysterious beginnings." In the unique Theater of Epidaurus, built harmoniously into the slope of evergreen-covered Mt. Kynortion, I listened to the all too perfect acoustics of the gathered crowd, but preferred the quiet of the crowd's dispersal. Surrounding hills seemed to cradle the amphitheater with a sentient care. I tried to inhale the freshness of a fourth-century B.C. land, but getting that peace of mind and soul wasn't easy. The distractions were everywhere, mainly in the form of tourists pumping up their egos. But despite the "bloody locusts," as one British couple described the crowd, the noise would fade every now and then, and one could hear the heartbeat of the land.

I returned to Nauplia. Earlier at the hostel cafeteria, I'd met an American artist named Glen who had just spent six months traveling in Africa. When I met him, Glen was reading the poems of George Seferis, a Greek Nobel Prize winner. He turned me on to lots of travel possibilities. Again I was overwhelmed by the choices here in Greece. The ring of legends was like a whirlpool in a draining river, big enough to suck me into its stem of mysteries. How would I cope? We decided to embark next morning for Tiryns and Mycenae. We talked about art and of traveling cheaply while attempting to absorb the truth of Greece by talking to the locals. Drinking retsina, I invoked Dionysus like a stoned poet, admitting I was just another bloody tourist, not a Greek wannabe. The myths would help me understand. So what if I was less than convincing? I stood in the ring of legends, shouting to a demi-god to join us for some wine.

The Argive Plain

Glen and I arrived at Tiryns before any other visitors. We entered the "cyclopean doorways" of Pindar's description and explored "wall-girt Tiryns," as Homer termed it. Settled as early as 3000 B.C., Tiryns was destroyed as a city-state by neighboring Argos around

458 B.C. The sky shone blue above the rough-hewn walls of giant stone, and a breeze with active warblers in the orange groves down below us lent a lively presence to the site. Glen explained that Greek citadels were often built in relationship to visible mountain peaks with "V" formations between. The breasts of Gaia and the mother's womb were kept in sight. The citadels were ostensibly aligned with the source of life. With that in mind, I stood in an underground passageway and photographed the eastern mountains as seen through an opening of a wall.

The Argive Plain had been inhabited since Neolithic times and had been the stage for countless myths. Modern Argos had been constructed over the original city and was not a walker's paradise, but Glen and I hiked it trying to find a bus station in order to reach the Argive Heraion, the sanctuary of Hera, someplace about five miles to the north. The Greeks of Argos seemed to know very little English but tried to be helpful. The station always seemed to be "out there," close by, as indicated with a snapping of the forearm from a vertical position to the horizontal. We assumed the Greeks were saying something like, "*That* a way, fellas!"

We decided to walk the distance despite the heat and the city's polluted air. We stopped at a fruit stand at the edge of town. An elderly woman sold us locally grown oranges, grapefruits, and honey. Fresh food sustained our vision of the Heraion, which our guidebook said is "usually ignored by present-day travelers." That was all the more reason to investigate the sanctuary and to pay our regards.

We walked through fruited groves and past fields of artichokes and other vegetables, terrain reminding us of southern California. I didn't know it at the time but we were tracking the old route of an annual procession from Argos to the Heraion where, in the days of Agamemnon, special honors were paid to the patron goddess. But after four miles, no sanctuary-bearing mountain had come into view. I'd been trying to assist Glen by hauling some of his baggage in addition to my own pack, and the pleasant walk had turned into a dismal, overheated trudge. None too soon the pavement turned to gravel, the final tractor passed us, and the slopes appeared. After a lunch break, Glen walked up ahead and then reported that he'd found the site hidden in the groves.

We approached a small shack at the entrance. Through an open door we saw the guard snoring in siesta. An assistant sat sleeping in an aged truck nearby. No doubt the Greeks in general were a hard working people but when each day brought siesta time the lights went off. We imagined ourselves the only tourists for miles around and we had no intention of disturbing the sleep of our guards.

We heard the bells of unseen animals grazing on the slope above the ruins. The temple to Hera had been built on several terraces in the seventh-century B.C. and was known as one of the earliest structures in the Peloponnese. We explored the site and then relaxed with a long view across the plain. A breeze cooled the air and we watched a merlin hovering in front of us. Skylarks of uncertain species vocalized and fluttered high overhead.

Just outside of the sanctuary walls we found a solitary, excavated tomb-site and wondered if it had been dug by the archaeologist Blegen, whom we knew little about except for the quote in our guidebook:

"Blegen dug many tombs extending in date from Neolithic to late Mycenaean in the surrounding area." I entered the darkness of the tomb then turned around to look out at Glen who had already poised a camera at the gaping hole. The photo shows me, or someone like me, resurrected from a grave dating back to a dark and hoary age.

The temple to Hera once contained a famous statue of the goddess built from gold and ivory by the sculptor Polykleitos. The statue, long removed from the site, depicted Hera sitting enthroned with a scepter in one hand and a pomegranate in the other. Thousands of years later, Glen and I sat in the same spot where the statue had stood on a breeze-swept mountainside. Utterly ignorant of the time that we honored, we were nonetheless awed by something that propelled us to our feet, and that fueled us for the northward walk along the mountain to a place called Mycenae.

Like other ancient cities that were powerful and influential, Mycenae was situated on a mountain. We approached it from the south along Mt. Sara, stopping at the rough terrain of an impregnable "Chaos Ravine" that in old days functioned as a protective shield. We found our way through a wall of huge conglomerate rocks that reached to 18 meters in height and that had once lined the city's boundaries. We wondered how rocks of such forbidding size were hauled and hewed. Some Greeks of the later Classical era could not believe that mortal hands had done such work. Again, the words of Henry Miller: "I say the whole world, fanning out in every direction from this spot, was once alive in a way that no man has ever dreamed of. I say there were gods who roamed everywhere, men like us in form and substance, but free, electrically free."

By the time we reached the famous Lion's Gate and had a chance to photograph it, a whistle blew for closing time. We had only a few minutes for study, to grasp at an understanding of this burial ground for Agamemnon and his murdered companions and for other notables of Greek drama and intrigue. The Lion's Gate itself is almost square-shaped, three meters by three meters. Above the lintel over the monolithic doorposts is a limestone triangle with a carved relief believed to be "one of the most ancient sculptured works in existence," circa 1250 B.C. The lions had lost their heads to thieves more than a thousand years later. The extensive excavation work at Mycenae was started by the German archaeologist, Schliemann, and continues to this day. Our brief walk through the ruined city founded by Perseus was accompanied by a flurry of ghosts and murdered heroes from the Trojan War. We, too, had our time cut short.

Corfu

After our return to Nauplia, Glen and I bade farewell to each other and proceeded on our separate journeys. I rode a bus to Patras and welcomed the time to rest my blistered feet. I sat beside a native traveler who, like nearly every Greek male I encountered, fingered a bracelet of worry beads. I suspected that the beads promoted the release of personal tension and, for the larger picture, might work to ease the national tension, also. Using worry beads was preferable to picking one's nose or to bombing innocent foreigners. As for Patras, Glen had warned me to hang on to my wallet there.

In Patras I found that I had to wait more than a day to take a night-boat to the island of Corfu. I took a cheap room in the Hotel New York which, unfortunately, didn't offer much convenience or privacy. The city was just a holding tank for me. How different was the writer Henry Miller's experience here: "For the first time in my life I was happy with the full consciousness of being happy." He had a great hotel costing "about 23 cents a day." Half a century later, my room was of another order, and included a manager barging in with a female attendant.

Next day, while waiting for my six o'clock boat to the island, I decided that May wasn't a good time to be holed up in cities. I longed to be out in the wilds. To ward off the sense that I was wasting time, I concentrated on mundane tasks (stabbing French fries, draining bottle into glass, thinking of home, etc.) and acknowledged that it was good to have nothing whatsoever to do in an afternoon in Greece. I was regaining a bit of the Miller happiness. It was difficult to be fully in one place simply waiting for a move, but I welcomed the new sensation. I was starting to believe that my old self was seeping slowly into the land of Greece. I was learning stuff, hour-by-hour selecting one thing over the possible hundreds. To do so was an act of freedom.

Hordes of college kids exited and entered the sea-faring tub called the "Georgio." They were trafficking to and from the great romantic islands. At one point, while walking along the quay at Patras, I noticed that two young ladies were walking behind me. Suddenly, in unison, they both inquired, "Hi, howya doin', baby?" I think they were foreigners rehearsing for an English quiz or something. Later, I knew I was doing right when, sitting against a wall and reading a book, I looked up at a drunk who was stumbling by and cursing me for whatever reason. I was reassured that the world is full of small surprises.

On Corfu, the town of Kerkira had block on block of tourist businesses—diverse, wonderful, yet depressing. Carcasses of goat and pig hung in columns from the caves of butcher shops. "Gross," stated an American female whom I happened to be passing. There were all too many specimens of skinned or stuffed animals such as fox, mink, and herons. Caged wild birds fed a morbid fashion.

I sat in a restaurant watching horse-drawn wagons with their loads of freshly cut vegetables. I had hoped to meet a young American woman I'd befriended on the rooftop in Athens. She had come here to begin a new job, and she'd asked me to find her address at the post office after I arrived. There was no sign of her anywhere. I thought of her as I walked away, passing huge displays of slaughtered sponge for sale, passing two large sheep, their hooves tied together, trembling on a butcher's floor.

Ostensibly, Corfu was the setting for Shakespeare's play "The Tempest." Lawrence Durrell, in his book about the Greek Islands, noted that Shakespeare's "Sycorax" is an anagram for Corcyra, the island's older name. I traveled to Paleokastrika, a resort on the western shore, where the hills and ocean scenery are magnificent and bring Shakespeare's play to mind. Forestlands surround a small turquoise-colored bay that's framed by rocky promontories. It's a postcard setting with a lot of depth.

I studied an old monastery on one of the promontories. Durrell described it as dream-like despite the presence of tourists. Olive trees surround the promontory. Long ago, Napoleon had stripped off the last of the island's oak trees for his warships, an event that was followed by Venetians making recompense to islanders by offering 10 gold pieces for every grove of 100 olive trees planted. Some of these olive trees were centuries old. Corfu receives more rainfall than the other islands of Greece, and so enjoys a green Mediterranean landscape replete with a background of Albania's snow-capped mountains.

Laying on the cove, I was feeling feverish and sore-throated. The sun broke from an overcast sky and an Orphean warbler added its vocals to the pastoral atmosphere, but I needed to retreat and find a place to sleep. After an extended rest, during which I probably sweated a lot of poisons, I felt improved, so took a pained walk down the hill and back toward the cove.

I approached a saddled donkey tethered in a stand of olives. Feeling chilled by the lingering fever, I sat near the donkey in a crib of goat's-beard and magenta-colored flowers. The animal grazed indifferently for a while as I opened my book of Ovid and began to read the ancient tales. Then the donkey turned its head my way, its ears straining closer to this odd human who apparently had no work for it to do. I imagined it thinking... very strange, indeed... before it turned back to its grazing, and whisked its tail at a biting fly.

The Pindus

With my health improving slowly I rode the waves from Corfu to Igoumenitsa, a small port on the mainland at Epirus. I was close to Albania in northern Greece. I transferred quickly to a bus bound for Kalambaka, near the site of the famous Meteora. My eight-dollar ride for the hundred-plus miles was going to imprint the Pindus Mountains of Epirus in my head forever.

We passengers traversed mile after mile of mules and chickens and roadside shrines with their offerings of half-consumed wine or beer. We climbed a narrow winding road through barren peaks with clouds draped along their ridges. We basked in sunlight that strained through the clouds like a full moon after dark. We listened to instrumental bouzouki music seeping from the bus radio and sounding pleasant for a change. One almost expected some Greek John Denver to begin a lyrical "Almost Heaven, West E-pi-rus." Thankfully we got an alternative. For me, it was the flight of a booted eagle, Europe's smallest, sailing beside us for a while, keeping pace on the updrafts.

Considering the roadway's hairpin turns and lack of guardrails overlooking drop-offs to eternity, I felt that any moment we could all be booted eagles. Luckily for the passengers, Brown Swiss cattle and longhaired sheep roamed across the road at intervals keeping our driver on his toes and off the speed. Out the window I had glimpses of many things that touched me for a second or two, and that stirred a futile desire to linger in a kind of alternate existence: unidentified flowers, stone walls, and a woman washing clothes in a stream.

Near the city of Ioannina, we maneuvered through right-angle turns against a backdrop of whitened peaks. Dealing with loops and turns on the narrow road, our bus suddenly faced another bus, and each one had to stop then edge past the other. Thankfully the traffic was minimal. We stopped for spring water gushing from a snow-covered hill. Our ticket man stepped out to fill a plastic jug. A small flock of kestrels, also known as hobbies, hovered below us over the slope. I made a time check. In the last hour we had traveled only 28 kilometers.

A group of kids walked down a mountainside toward a schoolhouse that resembled an unfinished sawmill. Several boys sat near the roadside drinking what appeared to be red wine. We began to pass miles of ecologically ravaged hillsides, barren ground, eroded, and overgrazed.

We parked at a restaurant that also served as a station for the snowplows. I entered and bought a Greek chocolate bar. Sitting outside in the cool air of the evergreens I felt a gust a warm wind arrive, and with it came the call of warblers and the cry of hawks from high above. Icy water, chocolate, and the long vistas on the valley began to fill me deeply. A red-backed shrike, the first of many more to appear in the next few hours, caught my eye.

On the bus, an American passenger tossed a candy wrapper on the floor, then reconsidering her action, looked at me and picked it up. Unbelievably, she then tossed the litter out of an opened window, saying to me in embarrassment that she knows better but the Greeks all toss their garbage, so why not do in Greece as the Grecians do.

I had a clear look at another red-backed shrike. Its back was chestnut red; the hooked beak was as prominent as the black eye-band. Apparently common in the brushy lands of Europe and the Mid-East, the shrike took my mind off callousness.

In the distance I could see the monolithic outcroppings of the Meteora, though we were still some 31 kilometers from our final stop. The travelers began to talk excitedly, as if their ordeal would soon be over. We crossed the plain of an ancient sea-bed that eroded severely over the ages, forming the Meteora. Erosion had left high pillars of rock on which medieval monks constructed monasteries. The structures had given monks safety "between Earth and Heaven." In their sky-bound cloisters, accessible only by a system of pulleys and baskets, the monks could avoid the profane conflicts of their day.

Meteora

It helps to know the Greek language here. The driver of our long-distance bus did not know English; instead of dropping off his passengers at Kalambaka, as intended, he drove us all a mile beyond our stop then simply opened the door and made us walk back en masse. Then, in trying to cash a traveler's check, I entered a theater of frustration and comedy. The Meteora is a tourist site, but due to its remoteness the place doesn't see many visitors. Donkeys were the beast of burden. The white Egyptian vultures circled near the village; the weather was hot but comfortable.

Having settled in a campground, I began to hike toward the columns situated above the farm town. The braying of donkeys echoed off the vertical sandstone cliffs. A stone house had been built snugly against a cranny in the wall of rock. Outside the house was a long line of brightly colored clothes waving in the wind as if to say, "Everything's normal here; there's no way up or down, but that's okay."

Walking on, I heard the flowing of a brook inside a thicket and stepped off the roadway to investigate. Inside the thicket I could hear the complicated thrush-like call notes of a bird, and then another of its kind. Was it the famous nightingale? Seeing one of the slim russet singers I confirmed my hunch. It sang like a sophisticated mockingbird or thrasher—trilling, chirping, and fluting toward climactic crescendos. The notes blended perfectly with that of a brook trickling in an arid land.

As if the first nightingale wasn't enough, I heard another new creature echoing off the hills. I had often wanted to hear the diagnostic coos of the European cuckoo. The two legendary species sang out simultaneously. The cuckoo's plaintive notes made me think of Wordsworth's poetry and of Grimm's fairy tales; the nightingale brought to mind the great ode by Keats.

I was surrounded by elephantine, thousand-foot columns of rock, by rough pillars of sandstone on which the old monasteries were perched. Across the valley rose the snow-capped mountains through which I traveled. From this place of songbirds and pillars, I heard a shepherd leading his flock down from above. The sheep bells and the shouted admonitions to a dog were offset by the horn blast of a bus resonating from within the rocks. Vultures and kestrels circled near the summits of columns piercing a cloudless sky.

In a golden sanctuary of boulders and waist-high ferns, I seemed pleasantly removed from my usual realm. My company included honeybees and a long green lizard that scurried from a careful step. I sobered, then, at the sight of a rotting sheep that must've fallen from the heights.

I moved to a lichen-covered rock beside a deep ravine. One could wax romantic here, I thought. One could be lulled by the idyllic and sacred, imagining the life of Pan, piping on syrinx, the notes of which might actually be the nightingale and cuckoo's. One could play at being the wizard of thickets, a lord of the lumbering turtle and the frantic ant. One could live in a house a thousand feet tall and be partnered with a dryad lover. A gentle wind was coupled with the lamb's cry; the scent of thyme was blended with the sky. For a moment or two, the world was as simple as a cuckoo serenading a mate with its incomparable Bavarian-clock song.

It felt great to be out of synch with the times. Here all of nature seemed alive to the moment; the cosmos invited human beings to participate in its dramas, to relax in its dwelling of darkness and light. This nature was pagan with its source of wildness; it was safe in its modernity, and not under the duress of times long ago. I couldn't ask for more.

Two middle-aged hikers approached me while I sat in the comfort of a wild place, shepherding thoughts "between Heaven and Earth." Their "Kalimera" greeting betrayed an American accent. My "Hello" betrayed the mask of one who shepherds wild thoughts and animal nature. I walked from these betrayals and headed toward the road.

Next morning I woke from a rough sleep on the ground. After a late breakfast I began hiking to the Meteora. I climbed the steep stairway that tourist promoters carved into the pillar supporting Theophane's monastery. There, for seven centuries prior, monks had used basket and cable for transportation. In the stone entranceway I gathered my composure. Once again I could hear the cuckoos echoing notes among the storied columns. I was greeted by a small, quiet man who accepted my coins and guided me to the cloisters. We entered a chapel, frescoed and rife with Byzantine images including some peculiar Bosch-like scenes of serpents and devourers. Above the monastery's roof were carillons that occasionally were the source of great reverberation among these heights. Two other monasteries stood on separate pillars and helped to form a sky community inaccessible to all but resident monks.

My guide to the cloisters led me to a recently discovered cemetery once used for the burial of monks. Among the boulders and flowering irises was a songbird known as the subalpine warbler. Making my descent from the pillars, I walked by tourist buses unloading travelers who quickly formed groups for photo opportunities. In the land of monk and shepherd I preferred to walk alone.

In Kalambaka I found a cheap hotel with great accommodations, which I gladly accepted in preference to another night of sleeping on the ground. When Sunday morning dawned briskly, I decided to make one more visit to the columns. Climbing the roadway I passed a woman riding her donkey in the opposite direction. A male black-headed bunting (dark hood and yellow undersides) flew among the bushes at roadside, and a nightingale, exposed on its perch, sang a full-toned song of territorial claim. When I paused for coffee at a small café, I watched a jackdaw fly above a church and cast its shadow over a gleaming cross.

I came to my brook sanctuary underneath the Meteora. I built a little altar of stones by a pool. I placed a Greek coin on a gravel bed of the clear water and removed somebody's box of "Jet" laundry detergent from the pool. Setting my blistered feet in the stream, I listened to the birds and watched a butterfly. Then, removing my shirts, I reclined in full view of the vultures soaring overhead. Hidden from the tourist buses passing by, I felt like Narcissus looking at images in the amber pool. What I saw inspired me to implore the gods to spare this little niche on earth. And while they were at it, would they please bless the whole damn planet that we humans put at peril.

Before I moved on to my final destination of Delphi, I took some time to reflect on this journey. I knew that wild localities such as this were repositories for fictions and tales of might-have-beens, but the real things I encountered here were a part of who I was. I thought back to a moment during my last day in Athens where I'd found the sandal shop of the poet Stavros Melissinos. Cloistered in his little store in a vast "flea market" of the city, Melissinos sold the sandals that he made and which had given him some international acclaim. Apparently even the Beatles once bought their footwear in his shop. There I'd bought a copy of the poet's "Rubaiyat" poems, and Melissinos asked if he might autograph the book. That would be fine, I said.

And I thought of John Fowles' book, *The Magus*, which more than any other single source had inspired my travel to Greece. In a scene of the novel where Nicholas and Alison had made love near the summit of Parnassus (a place I would soon be visiting), there was a view "for a hundred miles in each direction... mountains, plains, islands, seas... all the old heart of Greece." And there someone had formed from stones the small Greek letters meaning "light." It was an exactness that I tried to reassemble in my own way with the little stones beside this pool.

I felt a motion near my shoulder. It wasn't that of a bird, although it could have been. I realized I had taken my "tourist guide" too much for granted and had forgotten him. As Hermes, the sandaled one, slipped away beneath the Meteora, I wondered if his footwear, with its wings and timeless leather, had been fashioned by a poet I had met along the way.

The Meadows

The Miller's House

I was living on the east side of the village looking out across the Shenandoah to the Blue Ridge Mountains. I resided there for several seasons while employed at a private school for kids with learning and emotional difficulties. I enjoyed my last year of work at the school but knew I had to move on in the fall.

The historic structure that I rented and shared with several companions was situated conveniently in a county park beside a refurbished grist mill. The Burwell-Morgan Mill had been constructed in 1785. My home, the Miller's House, was built in 1820 on the site of the original miller's cabin. The renovated house, along with the mill and the park-like grounds, had been recently purchased by the county historical society. The site was a comfortable place in which to live, and generally it was quiet.

A miller had been hired for the seasonal tourist demonstrations of grinding cornmeal into flour. The mill itself was an imposing structure—several tiers of olive-colored plank and stone. The tumbling mill-race was an offshoot of Spout Run, a rushing stream that kept a great turning-wheel in motion. Ivy and Virginia creeper formed a green beard on the stone face of the mill each spring and summer.

The house cellar was unusual. One entered it from the outside through a rough-stone passageway converging and then widening again, as if the builders had attempted to avoid big rocks or had prefigured some design for the space above.

Six-inch boards had been laid down for the floors. A second wing had been added to the two-story structure in 1875. When the house was renovated a century later, the antique character was preserved from its black-tin roof to its irregular clapboards, from its whitened walls to its dark-green shutters and redbrick chimneys.

My three housemates had a penchant for extended parties at the house and for late-night trafficking of friends and acquaintances. To a degree, I enjoyed participating in their social soirees, but their busy schedules had started to grate on my need for solitude and desk-time. Unsure of how long I could cope with my friends' activities, I was grateful for the comfort of the Miller's House and for the Spout Run peacefulness and its rippled waters that were said to be a spring-fed domain for trout.

Driving to work one day I stopped for a young hitchhiker near the main intersection of Millwood. He was black and poor and, as he said, collecting unemployment while supporting a separated wife and two children. He enjoyed the quiet village life where, "You can walk the street and drink and have a good time, and if the Man is called, it takes him 15 minutes to come from Berryville." I found it hard to empathize with my passenger, but his shear contempt for the local aristocracy was understandable. When we slowed down for an entry of a white Cadillac to the road, the rider exclaimed, "Better *move* that big white car, Mister!"

At Millwood I was living on an edge between some of America's wealthiest and poorest individuals. My closest neighbors were assorted black families, some of whom dwelled in shacks and trashed-out buildings just beyond our private drive. Within a mile of home, however, one could find the painted fences and the long driveways of the rich. Bass ponds shimmered by the stone-gate entranceways to the pillared mansions and the horse barns with pretentious English names. Racing horses and Charolais cattle browsed on the eroded fields.

Carter Hall, of Carter Hall Tobacco fame, was just across the quiet highway from the Miller's House. Its lavish structure had recently become the headquarters of Project Hope. One afternoon I cruised slowly through its property for the first time, noting the tall majestic oaks and other clichés of Southern aristocracy. The main hall with its grand Corinthian columns was flanked by separate but connected houses, and everywhere the trimmed magnolia trees shone as if with an inner light. A crow flapped from the green expansive lawn and flew toward the mountains. I was left alone, circling outward in my car, departing from the gold plate of society.

We were quick to arouse suspicions of the gentry who headed the historical society, as well as other rich folk living on the outlying horse farms and plantations. They were people ever conscious of the park's historical and financial value, and they no doubt viewed us as communal residents, perhaps with devious sexual and drug-related behaviors inappropriate for a high-toned image. Soon an emissary from the well-endowed society began to drop by on occasion, unannounced.

Granted, I'd begun to see a couple of my housemates as victims of a social wasteland filled with shallow dreams and restlessness, as blind seekers for substance in their lives, but we were hardly anarchists (well, maybe I leaned that way politically) or lawbreakers or even disputatious souls intent upon the downfall of the house and mill. In the eyes of the upper class we were black, as black as the families who resided all around the park in ramshackle homes, people who were neighborly though unmindful of our habits. In the eyes of the rich, we were tainted, shaded by impurity and sinfulness, our actions inexplicable, mysterious and unfit. At least, that's the way I viewed the situation back around 1980.

Frog Town

Someone had thrown a man's dead body into the river. The incident had apparently been witnessed and reported to authorities. It made the local news without a hint of where it happened or who the victim was. Heavy rains had raised the level of the Shenandoah River and hampered dragging operations. On a day off from work, I sat in a Blue Ridge bar that, as rumor had it, was close to the site of the body dumping. All the patrons were talking of the murder incident but no one, including Bob, the old proprietor who always wore a cowboy hat and smoked a pipe or cigar, made a stab at who the victim or the killer was. Here, ignorance on a topic of this nature implied that, ultimately, the event was serious and not meant for screwing up by way of accusation.

Theories were admissible, however. "I'll bet someone tossed the carcass in at Frog Town and by now the damn river's took it out of state and into the bay," offered Bob. I'd never been enthralled by the idea of rural homicide, but had always been romanced by a general mountain ambience, especially since my move here for employment at the school.

"Papers didn't say if the body was white or nigger," declared Shorty. He delivered National Beer to the roadhouse every Friday and, characteristically, drank at least one bottle's worth while gassing with the customers. John, a muscular acquaintance with a week's growth of beard, sat next to me and said, "Better stay clear of Frog Town. Down there all you got going for you is the color of your skin. Last year a hunter found a black guy hanging from an oak tree. Hell, he never even told his wife about it!" John laughed and swilled his beer, forgetting he had previously recommended Frog Town as the place to score some moonshine.

John asked if I had ever stopped there. I had. Shorty, overhearing us, exclaimed, "And he lived to tell about it!"

Sometimes in the spring I would drive to the old meadows near the place to watch the ritual flight of woodcock at their nesting territories and to listen to the whip-poor-wills. Other than what stimulated my birding interests, however, all I knew of Frog Town was its "grocery store."

John bellowed, "Know what their slogan is down there? *We import sunshine; we export moonshine!*" He'd revealed the slogan once before when I was interested in purchasing a little export for a taste of mountain spirit. I had driven to Frog Town and passed a string of campsites on the river, passed the summer homes of wealthy urbanites on higher ground and, finally, passed wooded gullies with trash heaps and burbling streams. In the hollow was an aging meadow with several ramshackle houses and a tiny grocery store.

"Shee-it!" roared John. "That grocery store—it's got one refrigerator with six, count 'em, six Safeway popsicles that the old guy throws away each summer and replaces." John Hadley was drunk, and not quite correct. When I was there inspecting the refrigerator, I had found the box opened, with one Popsicle gone. There were *five* Safeway popsicles inside.

"Ain't much in just yet," stated the gruff voice behind me. Turning around, I saw suspicious eyes peering down a high ridge of the old man's nose. I mentioned John's name, but it made no difference that I could see. I settled awkwardly for an old pack of Workingman's Tobacco that I drew down from a dusty shelf and paid for, never once intending to actually chew it. Exiting, I paused to look at the structure. Had it not been for the metal grocery sign, riddled by rust and shotgun pellets, the place could've passed for a poultry shack. If it served as a front for moonshine operations, it could not have felt more natural.

Remembering Frog Town, I thought of it as a story being told, and ran the risk of mixing up an actual experience with the stuff of Southern legend and cliché. I knew that I'd sat at Bob's and listened to the stories and conjecture, as if I were sitting in a meadow in the springtime with a beer and with binoculars, expecting to see the flight of woodcock. I knew that I had once visited nearby Frog Town in the hope of buying Shenandoah moonshine. But the sequence of events in real time tended to blur and jostle with the passing of each season and the interjection of related elements from other Virginia tales. And it's true. As sure as spring peepers chorused again from the marshy ground of the Blue Ridge, someone had thrown a body into the river.

Baptism

One morning I awoke to the sound of *a cappella* music. It was a warm Sunday morning in the spring, and the hum wafted through an open window from a place neither close nor far. The songs were decidedly incongruous with the typical ambience of English park and hidden Palladian mansions. Stepping from the house into sunlight I perceived a congregation of black people alternately singing hymns and listening to a voice that issued from the middle of Spout Run.

I had never before seen a true Baptismal ceremony. Barefoot and curious, I approached the congregation at the stream. I was the anomaly, the sole white face in a crowd of 30 to 40 worshippers. Where I had previously observed the antics of muskrat, beaver, and wood duck, and where I had tried in vain to prove the existence of brown trout in the run, I now watched a Baptist minister thigh-deep in the flow.

Another man, wielding a pole for support, ferried believers singly or in pairs from the bank. Two receivers gripped the candidates, hoisting each one into the air then dunking the body backward into deep water. Standing at the rear of the group, I listened to hymns such as, "He's No Stranger Now," alone and oddly fascinated.

After the congregation had dispersed, I walked along the stone wall lining the creek and then among the wooden benches and picnic tables. Sitting in catalpa shade, I noted the arboreal highlights, particularly the tulip trees, the firs, and the sweetgum. This was *my* congregation, and it grew as I looked down and absorbed the blooms of dandelion, violet, and sorrel. Aphids, swallowtails, and chimney swifts sang their own hymns of otherness from the air. I tried unsuccessfully to define the no-man's-land between description of a place and its reality. I had definite limitations—possibly transcended somewhat when imagining the role of the Burwell-Morgan miller through the ages, from the days of Colonel Nathaniel Burwell, the original eighteenth-century inhabitant, on down to whomever had been hired by the present-day historical society.

I had yet to meet the new miller, a young guy who'd decided not to live in the house I temporarily inhabited. I took some consolation from whatever shortcomings I was feeling by recalling that, despite the Society's suspicions about our household, I was recently offered an opportunity to become an apprentice miller for the upcoming summer season. The members had apparently gained some trust in me because of my position as a residential teacher at the school. At any rate, with help from my partner, and wife-to-be, I declined the invitation and informed the local group that we would soon be moving north.

Sitting at a picnic table near the Miller's House, I imagined myself immersed in a beautiful meadow. I could hear the heartbeat of this meadow and it sounded like the beat of water on a shore. I felt baptized in an ocean of the rich and poor, a great water of diversity, of human beings and of plants and animals almost beyond imagining.

Huntley Meadows

At the picnic table I recalled a place named Huntley Meadows. This green spot in the midst of urban north Virginia was close to the place where my future wife had lived. After my first visit to this 1426 acre marsh preserve, a lush island in a vast suburban sea of human life, I often thought of Huntley Meadows Park.

A primary feature of this park, undoubtedly one of the finest wildlife observation areas in metropolitan Washington, D.C., is a wetland with a half mile boardwalk and a wooden tower surrounded by botanically rich forestland and meadow. Visitors enjoy a fragment of the more than 200 species of recorded avian life and more than 300 wildflowers. Urban marshes are particularly endangered and, in the case of Huntley Meadows Park in heavily populated Fairfax County, also rare.

Created long ago by a meandering Potomac River, Huntley Meadows was once a portion of a large plantation owned by George Mason IV. Mason family ownership continued into the 1900s when the land was sectioned off for farms. 1500 acres were reassembled to create a base for dirigibles. Some of the land was taken over by the federal government to become a testing ground for asphalt road surfaces, and then a base for the National Guard's anti-aircraft gun battalion with a duty of defending the Capitol during the 1950s. The U.S. Navy drained the marsh and set up radio communication research before the land was finally abandoned as "surplus" around 1970.

Beavers swam back to the streams and pooled the marsh again. In 1975, President Gerald Ford designated the land as a public park for "recreational purposes in perpetuity." More recently, despite urban pressures to construct a major highway through the park, Huntley Meadows has become a fine example of what dedication in the fields of education and environmental preservation can achieve.

In a warm spring morning, azure butterflies looped the air on fragile wings; pickerel frogs "snored" from lily pad and sedge communities. Great egrets and a great blue heron stood immobile, fishing beyond a pool of water. Greater yellowlegs flushed suddenly from the mudflats where a river otter was reported earlier in the day. The migrants whistled a three-note *tu!* as they veered upward, turning toward their nesting ground in Canada. A Caspian tern, unusual for this marsh, flew in from the east and circumnavigated the larger pools, occasionally diving for a fish, its large size and blood-red bill creating a visual impact for the human spectators. A pair of huge snapping turtles, often seen reposing near the boardwalk, rolled and splashed the distant surface as they mated, fulfilling their design for continuity while enjoying reptile pleasure and hastening coots and grebes toward quieter coves.

I remembered looking for two birds in particular—the American bittern and the palm warbler. My first bittern flew across the marsh grass 50 yards in front of me and landed in vegetation where its camouflage produced an appearance not unlike that of a reed or a stake or even a developed skunk cabbage plant. As I stood alone in megalopolis I watched this heron through binoculars: it was the classic "freeze position" – the bill was pointed upward; the strangely situated eyes peered out for danger. I had waited years for this opportunity, and there it was, the serpentine head and neck turning slowly as it watched me, then to hunker down and vanish in the grasses.

I was a little early in the season for discovering meadow sightings such as the Virginia and king rails and the prothonotary warbler, but the migrating palm warbler was ostensibly in town. I was told that small flocks of the palm, a colorful, ground-loving, tail-bobbing migrant, had been seen recently in a far field of the park, and that's where I finally saw it. On a field edge near a cluster of pines and hardwood trees, the small bird with a streaked yellow breast, a yellow rump, and a rust-red cap, made an appearance. Several of the birds bobbed their tails as they fed on the ground, regaining strength for a flight to Canadian muskegs, inadvertently uplifting my spirit as I watched.

I returned to the marsh and its observation deck, passing several booms placed strategically along a stream to catch a pollutant recently found to be leaking from a tank buried by the U.S. Navy in the 1960s. Toxic effluent had reached this tributary of the marsh. Once again I was reminded of urban pressures and the role of marshes as a natural purifier, though these wetlands have a limit for abuse and accident.

I rose from the picnic table near the Miller's House and ambled toward the mill. Even here, a remnant of the wild was in the clutch of human society. It was like a small, writhing snake in the claws of a traveling hawk. At the mill, a mighty wheel was powered by a little stream.

Primitive Curiosity

Unsurveyed and Unassessed

Somewhere in his many fine books that deal with angling for Northwestern trout and salmon, author Roderick Haig-Brown speaks of "primitive curiosity" in relation to an outdoorsman's drive for satisfaction. The motivation at the heart of angling and exploration of the wild is basic and primeval. When it's consciously driven it is personal; otherwise this curiosity of the world-at-large is subliminal and belongs to the human race collectively, ingrained from the time when every adult was a hunter and a gatherer or dependent on this mode of living. I think I've seen it in myself—a primitive curiosity, born from long years as a fly-fisherman and an amateur naturalist.

After years of having an interest in the upper Genesee River drainage near my home, situated close to the western New York-Pennsylvania border, in particular with the Cryder Creek drainage feeding into the Genesee, I finally had a chance to assist the Fisheries Biologist of New York's Region 9 Department of Environmental Conservation. We were electro-shocking numerous small streams in this drainage to determine water quality and, especially, the overall status of wild brook trout—a native species struggling for survival against great odds imposed by introduced fishes and, in general, by the impact of humanity.

For several years I'd had the feeling that I wanted to fly-fish every trout stream in the upper river drainage, from the sources near Ulysses and Gold, Pennsylvania downstream to around Scio, New York. I was looking at about 80 streams throughout this region, ranging in size from step-across brooks to the 30 foot-wide branches of the Genesee, and I had fished or at least sampled every one of them but a few that remained inaccessible or not yet found. Recently I decided that the quest to fish every Genesee River feeder stream containing trout just wasn't reasonable, or practical. It made more sense to be *aware* of the streams with native brookies in them, to work with the Department of Environmental Conservation (DEC) and with old-timers that had fished the region, to ensure that an inventory of these waters was complete, so that the native fish would be accorded the protection it deserved. That's where my decision to volunteer as an assistant to the DEC crew entered the picture.

Whereas some of the trout streams that we sampled in the Cryder Creek drainage of the Genesee had been scientifically surveyed eight or 10 times in the past 85 years or so, others had never once been checked for water quality and the presence of brook trout. Some of the unchecked waterways were streams I knew about, as an angler with a fly rod, or were streams I'd been aware of and had not yet cast a fly upon—although I wanted to. My primitive curiosity was harnessed to the efforts of the DEC's electro-shocking unit in early September 2009.

"...DEC Region 9 fish staff, assisted by an angler volunteer, found a wild brook trout population in this previously unknown, unnamed water. This stream emerges from a small wetland at the base of a ridge and flows for approximately 0.5 miles through old pasture land before entering Cryder Creek. We sampled the stream near an old cattle crossing (culvert) about 0.15 miles above the mouth. The site was 230 feet long and included pools created above and below the culvert... The stream was about 12 feet wide, but this was not average for the stream (more like three feet). The stream bottom was quite heavily silted, with abundant vegetation."

The DEC's assessment of this first stream continued: "We captured three adult wild brook trout and one young-of-year (YOY) brook trout. Low numbers of YOY trout in the main stream likely result from excessive sedimentation and high embeddedness to the substrate. Another limiting factor on the brook trout population may be competition with other fish species. Generally high quality, spring fed brook trout streams only contain sculpin and blacknose dace. In this stream, we found several other fish species: creek chub, pearl dace, white sucker, and brook stickleback. The brook stickleback was an unusual find; however, the habitat appeared to be ideal for them.

"Based on the presence of wild brook trout in this stream, the stream should be upgraded to waterclass CTS (native trout present and self-sustaining)."

I had urged the DEC to sample this quiet, unimposing brook. I soon referred to it as "Lyle Brook," in honor of its previous landowner, who had helped Trout Unlimited with several tree planting projects in the area. Lyle Brook is not exactly fly-fishing water, but it's nice to have it included in the DEC's domain of concern.

Of the six streams we sampled that day, another unnamed water hadn't been inspected by the state since 1929, when only the mouth was surveyed because the stream itself was too low. We checked 200 feet below a road culvert, which was good brook trout habitat for the 11 natives we captured and released there, and also checked 200 feet above the road culvert, where no trout were captured, indicating that the road culvert hadn't been installed properly and acted as a barrier to fish passage. But again, based on the wild brook trout found here, it was recommended that the stream be upgraded to the state's CTS classification.

After our lunch break that September day, we arrived at another neighborhood brook in this wooded hill country that I'd been anxious to explore. Scott Cornett, Fisheries Biologist, and his survey crew began work on a section that was 12 feet wide and had an estimated flow of two cubic feet per second, a typically small late-summer flow. The conductivity reading for suspended elements in the water was normal for this area, and we captured five adult wild brook trout and three YOY brooks. That was near a small bridge on a state highway. Recommendation? Upgrade the water classification.

Studying his topographic map, Cornett wanted to sample one more site in the headwaters of this little feeder stream (known officially as "T-13"). So we looked for wild trout at a previously unchecked feeder stream located on a hilltop. "The site was 75 feet long and included one good pool in the culvert below the road." Here the stream was only three feet wide and with an estimated flow of only 0.2 cubic feet per second. From that singular location (for which I cannot be more specific), we captured and released 13 adult brook trout in addition to mottled sculpin, creek chub, and sunfish. Very fine.

Spring Mills Creek

Spring Mills Creek is a major tributary of the Cryder drainage and I've been studying this little trout stream for years. Only several miles long before it drops into Wileyville Creek and then the Cryder, Spring Mills offers an opportunity to study and work with a system that is easily comprehensible and not so big that a remediation project on the water becomes a daunting project. Spring Mills had been stocked with brown trout until the early 1990s, but New York's DEC then realized that the small stream's native brook trout population had recovered well enough (despite the stocking efforts) that hatchery fish were no longer necessary.

About a dozen landowners hold property along this creek, and I knew if I was going to fish it and perhaps later do some habitat improvement on the stream I would need to introduce myself to them and talk. I've met most of the landowners and other residents of the Spring Mills community and found almost all of them to be congenial and supportive individuals without whose consideration I was going nowhere here.

Several of these people opened up their lands for my catch-and-release fly fishing for native trout. At one stream location I did small remediation projects like shoring up a fragile bend with rocks culled from the water and with shrubbery planted to hold down the soil. At locations in the headwaters and down near the mouth of the creek I pulled in the assistance of the Upper Genesee Chapter of Trout Unlimited which, along with other volunteers from adjoining communities, planted willows and other kinds of trees to eventually bring new shade and nutritional components to the wild fish and the other creatures of the stream habitat. Additional projects to assist the natural recovery of this creek and hill environment are in the works, but the process is of long duration and a challenge in every aspect.

Spring Mills Creek is a typical native trout stream facing hardships in the modern world. Whereas much of it has been stabilized as agriculture disappears from its banks and as forest cover regenerates, the headwaters have several newly established Amish farms that could be improved with better fencing so that livestock can't erode the banks unnecessarily. Erosion adds to the sediment that destroys gravel beds used for spawning.

Like most other native trout streams in the area, Spring Mills faces a variety of problems. Local highway departments need to be more aware of the damage they can do to gravel beds and of contributions they make in the way of run-off from the roads. Global warming brings new pressure to the cold stream waters that all native trout require; and the threat of mining in Marcellus Shale layers underneath the New York-Pennsylvania hills for the gas contained there has everyone who loves the natural beauty of this land concerned. The relatively new process of hydro-fracturing layers of underlying shale requires huge amounts of water typically drawn from area streams.

Several years ago I found that Pennsylvania drillers were withdrawing water from Spring Mills Creek in the autumn during a time of minimal flow and the spawning of brook trout. The resurgence of gas and oil drilling in this region has only just begun.

May Fly

One of my fishing grounds for August mornings is a trout stream close to home. Upper Dyke Creek is the habitat and spawning place for native brook trout and wild brown trout where the morning water temperature registers in the cool, low 60s. There one of the smallest of our mayfly order, *Tricorythodes* (or Trico, for short), is alive and well, inspiring the primitive curiosity of at least one fly-angler.

The daily appearance of late summer Tricos on this creek is almost so certain you can set your time piece by it. The adult Trico is an elegant centimeter in length, including its long sweeping tail. Adults tend to hatch from underwater nymph cases in the pre-dawn hours of a season that in New York runs from mid-July until the middle of September. Females descend to the stream to lay their eggs around 7:30 a.m., give or take half an hour depending on air temperature and water conditions. Minutes after the adults emerge, their bodies mutate into the breeding form of the insect known as a spinner. A mating swarm of spinners is often seen hovering above the stream, undulating in a horizontal movement parallel to the water. Usually the male spinners are higher in the swarm than the females which descend to lay their eggs, completing a life-cycle.

Trout will rise and sip at these winged morsels with a daily regularity that delights a fly angler with an otherwise limited opportunity to fish the local streams in this season of warmer waters. Most August mornings during my summer break, I can start off leisurely, have my breakfast and coffee, and make it to the stream in time for Trico action. Dyke Creek is a feeder stream to the Genesee River where, unfortunately, the water temperature often warms too much by August to allow good trout fishing. Upper Dyke, spring-fed and shaded, but not without its share of problems, tends to remain cool enough to fish throughout the warmest days, a fact I don't mind mentioning because, frankly, the stream is under-fished by folks who wield a fly rod and return their catches.

The late George Harvey, a famous Pennsylvania fly angler and instructor, studied *Tricorythodes* as early as 1927 and spread the word about the insect's possibilities, but for decades the diminutive fly with the big morning hatch was mostly ignored by anglers. It was written off as too damned small to fish with. Then, as catch-and-release fly fishing grew in popularity and as fishing seasons were extended later into autumn (a time when Tricos continue to appear in many places), anglers took more notice of the fly and started to enjoy casting with the tiny hook that Trico imitations require.

Usually when I fish the Trico hatch I cast an imitation of the spinner form. The wings of the spinner are tied in "spent" formation, or flat to the surface. It's produced on a sliver of a fly hook, size #22 or 24, using black thread for the body and three dun-colored (bluish) hackle fibers for a tail, splayed slightly. For wings I tie in a twist of Poly-yarn with a figure-eight wrap and then tie off the black thread at the eye of the hook. That's it, a minor operation but it's all done under magnifying lens because, believe me, the hook is tiny, about the size of one consonant appearing in this sentence.

I've heard anglers moan about the Trico casting because the fly is so difficult to see on the water. Usually they're the ones who haven't yet given it serious attention. My aging orbs no longer have the best of vision but I've never had much trouble tracking the drift of a #22 hook on the water, even without my glasses on. The white Poly-wings of the Trico imitation easily reflect the dimmest of morning light.

The Trico fly is generally cast onto a calm, clear flow. The average angler interested in mayfly imitations is able to track it readily and stay prepared for a gentle strike to the rise of a feeding trout. I said "gentle" because the fly is ordinarily tied to a very fine tippet (I use 6x or 7x) on a long tapered leader (usually a nine-foot minimum). I said "gentle" because the morning hatch is basically a time for peacefulness and quiet meditation, a time for one of the most relaxing and exacting aspects of the sport. By contrast, I find that the evening hatch somewhat earlier in the season, as exciting as it often is, can be frantic.

Tricos are a lovely fly, as small and fragile as the world of nature will present. Their imitations can unlock a primitive joy.

Living in Springs

Over the Volcano

I took the morning boat from Crete to Santorini. From the deck of the Orange Sun, a small Mediterranean cruiser, I watched the big Greek island, "cradle of the Western world," splinter to a memory in the haze. Water on the port side of the vessel was a dark blue wash that turned to turquoise in the sun.

One illusion offered by the sea is that of sameness, or the lack of diversity, spreading over everything that's seen or known. So it's up to the passenger's imagination to recover the variety of life beneath the roiling surface. An ocean is a lubricant of dreams, a perfect complement to the solid ground where I was headed.

Listening to the engine's purr, I also heard the hammering of crewmen down below the deck. Seabirds flew behind us and occasionally one or two would settle on the waves to rest. And no wonder they should follow: I heard a thud, then another and another. I was jarred at first, thinking that perhaps my pack had blown off to the sea, but no. A string of plastic garbage bags unfurled in a line behind the ship, a long, oily string of trash bobbing out behind us, soon to sink down to an otherwise beautiful realm beneath the surface. Out of sight out of mind, but I found the act of ocean trashing more offensive than illegal trashing of the land. On land, at least one can see the rotted fruit of our myopia and be forcefully reminded of our shortcomings. Anyway, I was glad to reach the storied land of Santorini.

Around 1500 B.C. a huge volcano blew its stack from what many people believe was the legendary island of Atlantis. The explosion left behind a hole that would become a harbor, the blue liquid mouth of a volcano 35 miles wide and 1,250 feet deep. Above this harbor stands the whitewashed village of Thira, the principle tourist town of Santorini.

A dilapidated bus took me up a winding, narrow roadway and the driver gave an oncoming truck plenty of audible warning, but the two vehicles met at a curve and had to halt. Each driver yelled at the other for a while. Ultimately the driver of the water transport had to fold down his outside mirror and edge his vehicle off the curb so we could pass. The tight squeeze was a prelude to my passage into otherness.

The village above me seemed ethereal. White architecture with its soft Byzantine curves reflected Mediterranean sun. Blue doors and window frames invited thought, and I entertained images of salt and coolness. I took a room from a hawker on a narrow street, a clean and private location somewhere in the alleyways of red volcanic cliffs.

A gypsy woman, blonde and rather unattractive, soon approached me with her dog. She said that she'd been traveling for at least five years, was having difficulty, and was wondering if I'd share my room with her. She'd become afraid to sleep alone. I felt sorry for her but told her I needed solitude. At that point my face was one that even I couldn't trust, so I wondered what I might've said had the traveling woman been attractive. I probably would've found myself quite ordinary.

For a while, walking the streets of Thira was like floating on a steel-blue sea. From this terraced old volcano I could look across the bay and see the ground beneath me as a jeweled desert island in the wide Aegean. Gulls that flew inward to the cliffs below were like notes wafting from a song of Earth. Water shimmered softly on the bay and a cruiser readied for departure. The volcanic harbor had a sweeping curvature that led my eyes away. A day would come when I thought of the departing ship as a fish—a colorful trout that flared gently over watercress in a faraway pool.

Thinking of the ship, I was reminded of native brook trout near my home across the ocean, of those white-edged fins in a cold pool of my favorite headwaters. *Fontinalis*, the trout's Latin name, means "living in springs," and here I could dream of living in such a world, even though what I saw in actuality was sun and pumice and blue water. Fresh water was so scarce in Santorini, such a precious commodity, that residents often caught the rain as it rolled off barrel-vaulted roofs into containers to be stored in some cool cellar. Water. Safe for drinking, great for dreams.

A scrawny cat approached me with a large rat hanging from its jaws. I wondered why a cat would bother with a beast of that size and, as I wondered, the cat jumped to the top of a low wall then down to a

93

grassy bank where I watched it settle in with a mess of little ones. Cat and kittens had a tasty island meal.

Two mules were prodded down a steep cliff to a small café. Each animal carried four cases of bottled beer. I heard the chatter of computerized games emanating from white alleyways. I worried that the Greek islands were running on borrowed time in their race for the tourist coin. I felt closer to the scrawny cat than I did to many of the tourists passing through. I bought whatever goods I needed from the working people and avoided the vendors of souvenirs. Earlier, while eating salad and drinking beer on the terraces above the harbor, I watched a line of mules and burros step down the infamous 566 steps to the harbor for yet another load of tourists to bring up. One of these tourists was the wife of a Hoboken, New Jersey executive. She was pleading for a hamburger cooked just right—"You know, American style!"

Another afternoon I witnessed several men pass by who looked like the Beach Boys of the 1960s wearing t-shirts reading "Columbia Pictures." They carried film apparatus and I learned that they were targeting set locations for the TV series "Love Boat." They were rounding up locals to serve as "extras." Corporate America was working on its notions of romantic Greece.

On the outskirts of Thira I took note of Spartan homes with thick cement walls, small windows, and barrel-vaulted roofs. Donkeys browsed in patches of daisy and thistle, one of them occasionally braying like the creaking of a rusty pump handle. Beyond them in the cliffs were small caves that once had served as homes.

In a large café I watched a young woman pause from her waitressing duties. She was from the state of Washington, she said, but she could've passed for a Greek with her dark hair and angular lines. She glared at the overbearing sun and exclaimed, "Whew! Make it stop!" and then she retracted her words, adding, "No! I take it back!" as if acknowledging that in Greece anything is possible, and that your words could be heard and acted on by gods and goddesses. I had placed several books beside me on a chair, and when the waitress finished her shift a short while later, she asked if I had anything she could read. I gave her my copy of Henry Miller's *The Colossus* and she took it, climbing on her rented motorbike and then driving toward the beach.

During my last day on this island I looked outward to a remnant cone of the old volcano. It was a black stub of lava close to the horizon and leaning toward the island of Thirasia. The island had three tiny villages still surviving without the benefit of electric power and modern conveniences. In that regard, Thirasia was like Santorini had been until recently. I felt the need to walk, so I descended toward the water and passed a number of little churches. The churches can be found over much of Santorini, but only a few are used with regularity. Most of them had been built by sailors who'd survived bad storms and vowed to build a church in thanks for being rescued, or else they had been constructed by wealthy individuals for their own personal reasons.

I rambled three miles to the sea without any further plan or destination in mind. Thira gave way to open fields with simple houses. Pumice and volcanic ash lined the pathway. Prickly pear, fig, lime, and lemon trees stretched out sparsely toward the blue. Lizards scurried off as huge formations of sand appeared. In an alien environment of red stone monoliths I started seeing caves, some of them obviously converted into homes or chicken coops. The walls along the path began to crumble, and I walked through bamboo groves. The strand was quiet and devoid of human life. A lark circled over the beach of black volcanic sand. I took off my clothes. The water felt warm—not as warm as the touch of blood from a minor wound, but more like the air.

Dog Canyon

"The Tularosa country is a parched country where everything, from cactus to cowman, carries a weapon of some sort, and the only creatures that sleep with both eyes closed are dead."
– C.L. Sonnichsen, *Tularosa*

One summer evening in New Mexico I departed from the Bosque del Apache National Wildlife Refuge and its green oasis with my wife, her father, and several other family members. This oasis in the desert country of the Rio Grande reminded me of the Montezuma Refuge closer to home in New York State, although the sandhill cranes had long moved on to their nesting grounds. Among my "life birds" at the Bosque, or first sightings ever (found with just an hour of frenzied birding in the heat), was an unusual neotropic cormorant, *Phalacrocorax brasilianus*.

We drove 100 miles across the storm-cloud spaces in the middle of the state. As curtains of rain were hung on the horizons, the clouds looked both promising and ominous. Monsoon weather had hit us and the pleasant smell of desert rain was in the air. Fine blends of color washed across the sky like paintings of O'Keefe observed in a museum. Traveling east toward Alamagordo we traversed the "Valley of Fire," a volcanic outflow measuring about 160 miles long and 30 miles wide. At one point we were near the Trinity Site, location of the first atomic bomb blast in the 1940s. We rested at the home of my father-in-law and his wife, Terry. Next morning, my son, Brent, and I began our planned hike on the Dog Canyon National Historic Trail starting at Oliver Lee State Park.

Traveling the approach road early in the morning, we counted 17 jackrabbits and desert cottontails. This would be my second climb of the Dog (the first had been seven years earlier). Our destination today was the Fairchild Line Cabin, a small stone ruin at the box end of Dog Canyon, almost three miles away on a very steep climb. We made sure to carry plenty of water for this summer climb of an imposing escarpment of the Sacramento Mountains. I chose my small 4x binoculars rather than the heavier 10-power glasses, though at times I would regret not having the stronger vision, particularly when trying to view the bird life near the spring-fed canyon.

There was no shade or protection from the sun along the lower half of the Dog. Sounds were easily transmitted. Brent and I would see no other people till returning to the small state park. From the trailhead we ascended the first 600 feet in four-tenths of a mile, placing our steps carefully to avoid disturbing rattlesnakes. At the first bench, or plateau, we marveled at the view of "insignificant Alamagordo" down below, beyond our campground at Oliver Lee, and out beyond the Chihuahuan desert-shrub community that surrounded us. As we continued on the trail we tried identifying some of the plant life here: mesquite, creosote, ocotillo, agave, century plant, horse-splitter cactus, and prickly pear. At times the narrow, well-defined trail had built-in rain diverters and a stone bench built for rest.

While still on the first plateau we paused again, for the sun had risen quickly, and viewed the canyon stream below. From our south side rose the sheer cliffs of dolomite and sandstone, outcrops of 1500 feet in a perfect silence of day, punctuated only by the call of birds. We were reminded that this vast, clean country in the mile-high Sacramentos launched itself upward from the Tularosa Basin. The magnificent scenery came with a price, for the land could be merciless in the sun, and often languished in a "skin-cracking drought."

In our walk toward the second bench we switch-backed into grasses and a fragrance of scattered juniper and ash trees. Until the previous day the Lincoln National Forest of New Mexico that embraced us had been closed to the public due to "fire hazard," but now we walked this trail alone through an open stairway to a fresh empyrean. It was big land with a big sky overhead.

It was easy to see how the canyon water had sliced through these mountains, how its trail turned and twisted through the multi-colored cliffs. The Spaniards had called this section of the Sacramentos the Canon del Perro, the Canyon of the Dog. It had been travelled by the Mescalero Apaches who knew it well. It was said to have the finest water in this desert region, water that trickled down a canyon from the rim of which we could peer westward and see the great White Sands.

An enormous black ant, or a beetle, with an orange abdomen, scuttled from the trail. A male Scott's oriole perched on a tall cactus stalk and warbled its loud, sweet notes across the arid slope. Brent and I observed the black and yellow songbird through binoculars, and then saw an uncommon black-chinned sparrow as white-throated swifts fed busily in the canyon air beyond.

At the second bench we dropped down to the top end of the box canyon through large junipers and cottonwood trees. We were half way to the pine-clad summit, and the trail was far less precarious now. Beyond the Fairchild Cabin, and beyond what we would try today, the trail became a tenuous thread, a steep ascent known as the "Eyebrow Trail."

The first cattlemen and white explorers of the region coveted the springs of Dog Canyon. Francois Jean Rochas, also known as "Frenchy," was a hermit short in stature who settled in this wildest section of the Tularosa Territory in the 1880s. He built a stone hut where the mountain water brought its sustenance out upon the valley, where Apaches had been known to camp until recently. Friends had warned the bald Frenchman not to do it, not to set up alone in such a wild place, but the European with a wind-red face insisted. According to C. L. Sonnichsen, author of *Tularosa, Last of the Frontier West*, Rochas "loved solitude and found comfort in the savage scenery around his tiny hut, the burning desert beyond his door, the remote menace of the pale blue sky over his head." Friends of the hermit warned him to at least file a claim to the place, but Frenchy never felt the need, saying that he was at peace and would be well. Throughout his decade at the canyon's mouth, Apaches never gave him trouble, but the cattlemen did.

Frenchy's water at the shielded site was "cold and pure and plentiful," especially loved in the years of drought, and Brent and I also enjoyed the miniature flow of liquid gold, the trees and grasses sprouting from its flow. But we had climbed well above the Rochas site with its vestige of a long stone wall and orchard, the place where Frenchy was murdered in 1894.

At the Line Cabin ruins, with its open roof and side and rusted bed frame, we had gained 1500 feet in elevation along the trail. While we rested for 15 minutes, I heard the dove-like coos of a whiskered screech-owl, which I later identified as a life bird for me. It is "common in Southwest canyons," according to my field guide, though its home range is apparently small. While the stream gurgled through heavy vegetation, and while we spoke with few words, the owl's notes were amplified, echoing from the steep rock walls.

The Eyebrow Trail, above us, wasn't meant for summer climbing; we would have to try it in a different season. The trail, an extension of our Dog Canyon path, was known for a special feature. It was used for ambush.

When Apache Indians were pursued closely by their foes, they would scramble up the trail here and wait for the enemy. As their foes approached, Apaches wiped them out with a shower of rocks and arrows. As the writer Sonnichsen put it, Apaches "took delight in listening to the screams of men and horses plunging into the depths below."

The Apaches had fought off the Mexican Army here, as well as the United States Cavalry, on at least three occasions. The last battle was fought above the spring on 18 April 1880 when Captain Henry Carroll and his Ninth U.S. Cavalry were ambushed by Apaches and swept away beneath a rain of boulders.

Many men perished for want of the Dog Canyon stream. They wanted its water for cows; they wanted it for personal comfort; and they wanted it to wash out gold in order to get rich. Like other desert canyons with a more or less permanent flow of water, Dog Canyon's life blood entered a basin and quickly evaporated in the sand, beyond the grasp of early settlers. For a while, the French hermit lived pretty well at this location. He would buy whatever supplies he needed in Las Cruces and then cross the grim Tularosa Desert 65 miles to his home. It was said that Frenchy was the first man of the territory north of El Paso to grow his own salads and have an orchard. The true-life story of his betrayal and murder by Tularosa white men makes an interesting tale best left to the curious researcher.

On the day that followed our climb into Dog Canyon, I made an evening visit with the family to White Sands. We listened to a ranger speaking of the 275 square-mile National Monument and watched him make a laser-point demonstration on the first stars appearing in the night sky over these dunes of pure white gypsum. He explained the constellations and their cultural significance. Behind him in the west, the San Andreas Mountains faded from a bluish dome. A crescent moon shone above. The shifting white sands felt cool beneath us where we sat. Each grain was like a star in a universe of gypsum sands. The ranger said that if you placed an orange on the sand before you and imagined it was the sun that gives life to our planet, then the next nearest star, Alpha Centauri, would be another orange situated in downtown Mexico City, hundreds of miles from where we sat. He was good at placing our humanity in the context of an indescribable space.

I sat there thinking of how distant the world of trout and fly-fishing seemed to be. I thought of it as a world entirely lost, but then I looked up to the Milky Way, that band of pale light sweeping south to north across the darkened sky, and suddenly the cool air all around us felt like water, like the wash of a pure mountain spring. I thought of the stream flowing out of Dog Canyon nearby, how it nourished the wildlife I had seen there in the park the evening before-- the rattlesnake, the striped skunk, the verdin nesting in a mesquite bush, and the five "collared peccary," or javelin. Water meant everything here. And yet the water inched-out over the flats and quickly vanished in the sand.

Subalpine

Bavaria

On a southbound train to Munich and beyond, we traveled through a forest then beside a lumber yard and a village where the train rumbled to a stop. Soon, two adults with a young boy joined us in our booth. The kid was around five years old. His appearance (aside from the plastic eyeglasses set in green frames) startled me in the way he looked like I did at his age—with round head, fat cheeks, and behavior all too regimented. His parents read *Kicker* magazine (mine were never so sports-oriented, other than sharing an interest in baseball). The ride became unsettling as we sat near this kid who wore shorts and sandals, as I noticed how he cocked an arm at his side or straightened out a leg. It was like revisiting a time and place that threatened to derail whatever journey I was on in the present.

We arrived at the resort of Berchtesgaden where, in the early 1950s, my parents managed a chalet-styled hotel. The mountain air was crisp and clear, the streams and rivers sparkled, and a few of the August peaks had snow on them. It was a German holiday, unfortunately, and we scrambled for a place to stay. It was late and we decided risking a side trip to Salzburg, Austria. There we found a good room at 450 Schillings.

We had been here briefly just a week or so before. We were more relaxed on this occasion and toured the old romantic city at our leisure. Drinking a beer at the café beside the castle, Bebe and I unwound before an evening panorama of sunlit mountains. We were heading in the right direction, after all.

Next morning we returned to Berchtesgaden. Now the sky was clouded and the air was hazy, and although the tourist town was crowded, it was pleasant being there. We bought a ticket to ride on the fabulously emerald waters of the Konigssee ("King's Lake") with its sheer mountain walls that echo a boat conductor's trumpet notes when the vessel is stilled and drifting silently. As our boat edged by the famous St. Bartholomew's Church, an artistic Byzantine structure, I glanced beyond the vaulted architecture to the Watzmann, an imposing mountain that rises as if from edges of the lake.

We stepped from the boat at the south end of the Konigssee and walked through alpine meadows to the Obersee, a second lake as beautiful as the first. Back in those days I was even more of a romantic than I am now, three decades later. The splendid scenery rippled an unfamiliar pool of tenderness inside me, and I proposed to Bebe that we marry and transcend the yin and yang. It was planned, of course, for a moment in the Alps. Actually I'd been thinking to spring the question while riding a chairlift to a mountaintop, but traveling on the lake was taking longer than expected, so I thought to make a fool of myself right there and then.

We did take a lift (Jennerbahn) to a stunning height, drifting upward slowly over the firs and flower carpets to a point where light rain began to fall and the air felt suddenly cool. At a small shop there we consumed a slice of cheesecake with tea and coffee while enjoying the views which, clouded at times, were overwhelming nonetheless. We wandered the tourist paths over the slope, passing a shepherd cottage and ski huts. The supreme beauty here was marred only by a surplus of people like us. Again we peered across the valley of the Konigssee to the grand peaks of the Watzmann, thinking how a visit here in the off-season when the weather is clear would be even finer. When we reached a mossy outcrop we discovered a wooden cross, perhaps for a climber's death, and several Alpen drohe, or alpine choughs, which are crow-like birds with bright yellow bills. The choughs flew slowly by us at close range. By request, I repeated my marriage proposal to Bebe, and again this fine young woman from Virginia foolishly accepted.

The alpine ambience must've been acting on us like a mild hallucinogenic. The experience had me tripping over verdant meadows through the fir-clad mountains. We heard cowbells clanging from little farms with rushing streams nearby… Three months later, in the U.S.A., our engagement was annulled, and our three-year relationship sadly ended in a mess. Ah well, thanks to alpine moments here and there, mundane existence is a time for paying dues.

Marble

Our campground at Bogan Flats was situated in one of the most scenic alpine valleys of the Colorado Rockies.

Its Crystal River flowed beneath 12,000-foot peaks named Elk and Chair. Elk Mountain belonged to the Snowmass-Maroon Bells Wilderness, and Chair was located in an area known as the Raggeds Wilderness. The Crystal offered trout fishing as close as 100 feet from out tent.

It was early August and I was here with my family visiting the camp host, who was my father-in-law, and his wife Terry. My son and I took an introductory walk down river and saw a golden eagle flying over the narrow valley. Broad-tailed hummingbirds whistled by or rattled up close to the red parts of our clothing. Bluish, vase-like flowers known as explorer's gentian blossomed in the mountain meadow.

Down river, en route to Carbondale where I would buy my Colorado fishing license, we stopped at Redstone, a pretentious village that had excellent pie and ice-cream and an overabundance of expensive mini-sculptures fashioned out of pure white marble that was quarried some miles above our campground. Black-billed magpies and black-headed grosbeaks flew against a background of attractive red canyon walls.

The Crystal River joins the Roaring Fork, a Colorado River tributary, at Carbondale. Upstream on the Fork, toward Aspen, the famous Frying Pan River pours in—all of which create an excellent trout fishery, enough stimulation to keep a fly angler like myself involved for a lifetime. I had plenty to do near camp so, aside from a few hours spent casting near the sagebrush and cottonwoods of the Roaring Fork, that's where I would do my fishing.

In the afternoon I walked the Placita Trail on a slope below our camp. It was a hot climb so I quit in the coolness of aspen woods and saw my first western tanager. Across the valley rose magnificent Chair Mountain, which my young daughter described as a "tilted baseball stadium in the sky." It reminded me of a blown-out volcano, also slanted, with a more traditional cone shape out beyond. Later I visited Avalanche Creek, whose narrow roadway had been recently cleared of... an avalanche. I walked a dry gulch where eroded sandstone took the form of reddish pillars and a steep landscape worthy of coyotes, bear, and cougar. Across the boulder-studded cutthroat water on the north side of the canyon, desert gave way to an alpine habitat with conifers and aspen.

Walking up the fast-flowing creek I stopped at a deep hole and refreshed myself from the heat and grime by dropping into the frigid water like my old friend the American dipper that flew in for a brief visit. Back on the roadway, where the red mud of a slide had baked in the sun, I inspected paw prints of bear and coyote as a Stellar's jay squawked nearby.

One morning on the Crystal, near the hamlet of Marble which is overlooked by the mighty Chair, the fishing was excellent with dry flies, particularly with attractor patterns Royal Wulff and Adams. A 15-inch brown trout with a coppery sheen and a deep buttery-toned gut was captured and released. I faced the challenge of a small deep hole with rushing water and conflicting surface currents. Stream willows edged the borders, but what spurred me on was a large rainbow that rose and struck at the fly, missing it several times before I devised a new strategy. Approaching the trout directly from the downstream side, I saw the rainbow lift and slam the fly again. This time it shot away with the line, and I had to stumble down through a rapid, boulder-strewn river, holding on while trying to work the big fish into the quiet shallows below.

The fine mid-day fishing in the Rockies required a "reality check" every once in a while, like a pinch to assure myself I wasn't dreaming. Looking up, I took in the rocks, the mountain, and the White River National Forest country where I could hear occasional hammering sounds. New multi-million dollar summer homes were rising at the edges of the forest where the process of "Aspenization" (the resort wasn't far off) chipped away at the beauty and sense of solitude. Returning to my casts, I thought about the wild, leaping character of the rainbows I was catching. The fish seemed healthy as I brought them to hand, despite the problem of Whirling Disease. There had been no stocking of the river for at least a few years, and that had helped to ease the fishing pressure.

I began another morning by riveting my attention on the currents as brook trout after brook trout, wonderfully colored, rose to the fly and got a brief inspection. After a mid-day break, and later, after fishing out the evening for brown trout, I knew I'd made a personal record to that point in my life-- a catch and release of over 40 fish in one day.

Marble is a small frontier-tourist town located at an elevation of 8,000 feet. The place has a general store that's ringed, on higher ground, by expensive summer homes, but Marble is basically known for its once great quarries and an industry that now attracts a lot of people with artistic inclinations. The world's purest chunks of marble, some of it car-sized, lie scattered over the ground and on the river banks. Local rock has been sculpted into famous Washington memorials and continues to be marketed in Italy as "Italian marble." A young boy stood beside the gravel roadway holding up a sign for passers-by: "Lemonade on Marble." The road to the quarries was posted: "14 known avalanche areas can be found on this road." My old Suburu, wanting to climb this roadway to the cutthroat fishing on the Crystal's headwaters, deferred to the Jeep and four-wheel gang.

The Crystal, in its little canyon there at Marble, looks deep in places, as clear as water from a kitchen tap, and flows on a bed of rounded stones of various color (frequently white) reflecting brightly when the sun is out. This mountain stream, spectacular in places, remains one of the last rivers in the West without a concrete dam. Sometimes I would wade up the middle where the width averaged 50 feet to cast toward the bank on either side, but I did so carefully—wading can be treacherous on the rocky bed.

I caught my first mountain whitefish here, a large species related to trout but looking more like suckers—slimy and scaled—with a tiny mouth that readily demolishes flies. They weren't as much fun as trout, but added to the interest where conifers scented the air and dippers flew from rock to rock.

Above Bogan Flats there's a campground reserved for groups such as Boy Scouts. There, on a Monday, I was the only one around. I shared some space with dippers, mule deer, ravens, elk, and (potentially) bighorn sheep or mountain goats above me on the slopes. At the head of the main pool near this camp, I found the paw prints of a bobcat, each print two-by-two inches with the toenails clearly indicated.

As snow continued melting from the heights of Chair to trickle into the river, I saw a large trout in a backwash created by a boulder. I dropped a fly above its window and watched the big fish rise. I set the hook gently when I should've been more forceful. I'd been used to hooking fish in the fast water where a gentle raising of the rod tip was all I needed. Here I felt the hook strafe bone, and a 20-inch rainbow merely spit the fly back out. I blew it. All I could do was slink away to catch nice brook and rainbows just below, but nothing could compensate for my failure with the hefty one.

At one point near Redstone I stumbled on a bull elk at the river, an impressive animal with velvet-coated antlers. Soon a cow appeared and joined him, the first of many western elk that I would see through the years. That evening I took my daughter fly-fishing for brook trout at a pond near Marble and we enjoyed casting over the cool spring waters.

Occasionally a fisherman or two would stop and fish this alpine valley with its daisy grasses and blue sky overhead, but they seldom worked with artificial flies. Most potential anglers spoke about fishing the "Gold Medal" waters of the Frying Pan and Roaring Fork, but I imagined those valleys being hot and crowded now. The Crystal was public and unpressured and of lesser status, though at one time it was ranked among the best.

As I neared the 150 trout mark on my tenth and final day of fishing the Crystal, I approached a favorite stretch, an isolated spot that I referred to as the Burnt Tree Pool for a large tree that had been struck by lightning. The sentry-like specimen, a ponderosa pine, had once leaned vibrantly toward the river's 200 foot-long pool, and was now a rusty-colored ghost with a double trunk, a startling presence on the Crystal.

Several days before, with my first attempt at the pool, I'd hit a "grand slam" at this location. That is, I caught four species of trout in the pool, plus whitefish. The new trout was a cutthroat of about 12-inches length that rose from behind a boulder in the water's tail section. Most of the river's cutthroat, with their orange gills, spotted sides and bluish marks around the eyes, were beyond me in the headwaters, so this was a welcome sight. I would catch only one more of them from the Crystal.

I made a roll cast toward the bank and placed an artificial grasshopper at the water's edge. A heavy rainbow hit the fly and tore up the pool, peeling off line until the fly popped out, the hook nearly straightened. River hatches were sporadic but strong for the remainder of the afternoon and evening; and the fishing was adrenaline-pumping with the use of different dry fly patterns. Even the whitefish, streaking from mid-stream boulders like a reddish flame, tried to burn me with excitement.

It was family that had put me on this river. And when I thought of Elk Mountain, Chair Mountain, and Burnt Tree Pool, when I recalled Avalanche Creek and Marble village, I knew all of them were more than places; I had eased my way into their slopes and waters; I'd slipped into their frames and shadows, and come to know them as a family of forms.

Greenback

The greenback is one of 14 subspecies of cutthroat trout (two of which are now extinct), each one rather neatly segregated from all others by the geologic boundaries of river basins. The greenback cutthroat trout is found primarily in Rocky Mountain National Park in Colorado, and it was there—in the Visitors Center—

that I beefed up my information on the trout before my wife and kids and I set out to find it.

The park's alluvial fan along the lower reaches of the Roaring River is a remnant of a serious flood occurring years before when a natural dam on the mountain collapsed and flushed its lake of water, killing several tourists and campers. Today the fan was a sunlit cascade of water in which we spotted greenback trout apparently indifferent to everything except their spawning interests.

Cutthroat trout are very sensitive to changes in water quality, especially to increases in sediment and water temperature due to grazing, logging, and road-building, but these greenbacks, the state fish of Colorado, originally native to the headwaters of the South Platte and Arkansas rivers, didn't seem to mind the presence of tourists. Highly vulnerable to extinction (particularly due to hybridization with rainbow trout, an introduced species throughout the Rocky Mountains), these greenbacks allowed our careful approach with the camera. My wife, Leighanne, took a nice photo of an olive-colored specimen, even capturing some of the dense black spots and red-orange coloration at the gills and fins, by slowly submerging a digital camera in front of the fish.

With a family drive over the continental divide on the highest through-road in the U.S., we stopped near the tundra habitats of elk and marmot where my son and I pitched snowballs at each other. Then, descending from the realm of 13,000-foot peaks, we paused to explore the banks at Hidden Valley Creek where I also decided to suit up and fish for greenbacks. Here, too, the casting for cutthroat trout was on a catch-and-release basis only, with the use of barbless flies.

The greenback, *Onchorhynchus clarki stomias*, was declared extinct in 1937, wiped-out by effects of mining, over-fishing, and the introduction of non-native species (primarily rainbow trout). The fish was "rediscovered" in a few headwater streams in 1969 and was one of the first fishes to be listed by the newly created Endangered Species Act. Transplants of the trout into small isolated streams like Hidden Valley were successful, and eventually the trout's recovery in Rocky Mountain National Park became an icon for trout restoration efforts in this country. By 1978 the greenback was down-listed from endangered to threatened status, and catch-and-release fishing was allowed in the park.

Hidden Valley Creek is only a few feet wide where I sampled it, but it was deep with lots of undercut bank. The numerous fish were easily spooked, and all I caught were a few brightly colored brook trout. I had better luck at the lower end of Roaring River, where I approached it by a walk along the scenic Fall River.

On the Roaring's braided alluvial fan, well below the knot of summer tourists, I caught the first greenback on an artificial ant. It was small but unmistakable. I caught several more in the rushing water of the deeper pools.

Next day, following an evening dinner in Estes Park to celebrate my daughter's nineteenth birthday, we hiked a trail to Dream Lake where the high country promised one more shot at greenback fishing in a beautiful setting. Leighanne stayed with me at this glacial jewel while son and daughter hurried up the trail to Emerald Lake and the shadow of 14,000-foot Mt. Hallett.

With special fishing regulations here at Dream, I laid out a long cast to the rising cutthroats (highly selective fish, considering the angling pressure) and finally caught a male greenback measuring 14 inches. Leighanne took photos of the fish, and soon the kids returned with their own subalpine stories of a special lake and a mountain just beyond.

Green Fire: Homage to Leopold

Our plane landed in El Paso with a midnight wind and a temperature of 100 degrees. Headed for Alamogordo, New Mexico, we braced ourselves for drought and summer weather unusual even by southwestern standards. Forest fires had already raged across western Arizona and northern New Mexico and at the moment were flaring up in the Sacramento Mountains near Alamogordo. We'd be staying with my wife's family on the outskirts of the city, but I was anxious to explore a cooler, wetter environment, hopefully north of Santa Fe. We'd learn that northern fires had forced the closure of public lands, so my wife and I began to look south and west. The Gila National Forest would be dry but green, remote and distant, and unknown by both of us. With the blessings of my father-in-law and his wife Terry, we departed from White Sands and the Tularosa Basin and drove to Glenwood, New Mexico near the Arizona border.

En route to the Gila I observed, ever so briefly, my first life-bird on this journey from New York—my first sighting of a Harris hawk, soaring over Interstate 10 near Deming, New Mexico. The raptor's diagnostic trait was a chestnut coloration underneath its gliding

115

body. We'd reserved a homestead cabin for three nights and would face the Mogollon Mountains and the Gila Wilderness. The renowned Catwalk National Historic Trail would be several miles up the road at Whitewater Canyon, and there I'd look for trout and wander through a birding wonderland where some 300 species of avian life could be found in a typical year.

The Gila was the nation's first designated wilderness, thanks to the early efforts of the pioneering author and conservationist, Aldo Leopold. The Gila, along with the adjacent Aldo Leopold and Blue wilderness regions, comprises much of a national forest system that includes one of the largest roadless areas in the Lower 48 states. Although the grizzly bear no longer roams the wilderness here, the Mexican gray wolf has been reintroduced, and bighorn sheep roam the higher altitudes. At first I was disappointed not to be cutthroat fishing and exploring in the Rockies north of Santa Fe, but I was starting to look forward to immersing myself in the Mogollons—at the southern rim of the trout's world in North America.

Following my purchase of a five-day fishing license at the general store in Glenwood (uncertain if I'd find enough water to actually fish in), we settled into our cabin grounds on a well-established ranch. Shortly afterward I found my second life-bird of the trip, the phainopepla, which resembles a big dark waxwing in profile, but with white wing-patches. It demonstrated a familiar flycatcher habit as it reeled gracefully from a treetop to snatch a flying insect.

Glenwood village is a small oasis in a valley with some wild American history and authentic airs. Several hundred residents host a bar, a few tourist shops and a general store, and give the visitor a base for rest and exploration. Our cabin site, one of several buildings on the ranch, was tucked against a rugged westward slope. Its air-conditioned rooms and modern amenities were a luxury not to be taken for granted. Although the hot Mexican climate could be brutal here throughout a summer day, the air is typically comfortable at night. The mountain air, and its smell, so difficult to define, was sweet no matter the hour, especially at our doorway with its table and chairs.

It was interesting to learn that the native Gila trout, one of the rarest of salmonids, was recently moved from the nation's Endangered List to that of Threatened status, thanks to the work of the Federal Gila Trout Recovery Team and its support groups. The Gila could now be fished for in select recovery streams, under special regulations. In another season, with more time for hiking into the remote canyons, it would be fun to fly-fish for this beautiful trout. For now, however, I was satisfied attempting to locate the more accessible hybrid species, the Gila-rainbow, in nearby Whitewater Creek.

Shortly after our arrival in Glenwood, Leighanne and I inspected the mouth of Whitewater Canyon where the Catwalk Trail begins and where the sycamores introduce a fascinating riparian zone. Storm clouds were brewing slowly over the Mogollons, and thunder rolled down the canyon slopes as if to announce commencement of the monsoon rains—none too soon, according to local residents. Parts of New Mexico hadn't seen rain in nine or 10 months. The first raindrops puddled on the dry creek bed, on the parking lot and on the hardpan roadside as we drove back to the cabin. Polly, our hostess, welcomed our arrival with hearty thanks for "bringing on" the first brief shower. With the smell of desert rain, one could almost hear the floral pores of creosote plants opening to grasp new moisture in the air. When these desert plants embrace the moisture they release a famous odor, one of my favorite southwestern sensations.

After an early morning walk near the cabin, viewing birds such as black-headed grosbeak, Say's phoebe, and acorn woodpecker, Leighanne and I visited the canyon. Among the first visitors for the day, we entered the mountains via the Catwalk, an excellent suspension trail that follows a historic pipeline path once used by silver mine employees from a mill that had been located near the present day parking lot. The Catwalk leads upstream through the canyon for more than a mile, at an average height of 10 to 20 feet above the Whitewater. Thankfully the creek, although intermittent for a while near the parking lot, had water in it—a cold, clear flow that strengthened as we walked. And pleasantly enough, the eye of this fly-fisher caught the sight of trout. Small quick motions in the limpid flow counter-balanced the rise of canyon walls, the heights of which were staggering.

Although the native Gila trout had been nearly exterminated in the 1900s through habitat destruction and the stocking of rainbow trout (with which the Gila readily interbreeds), the hybrid flourished below the Catwalk. Stalking with a fly rod I could wet-wade into the tails of Whitewater pools and catch them on a dry fly. The small yellowish trout were darkly spotted on their olive backs and had the parr markings of a rainbow. I released them in quick succession from the barbless stonefly pattern and returned them to their haunts. By observing wild creatures of the region—the mule deer, lizards, insects, and especially the birds and trout—I felt capable of entering the landscape and gaining access to its spirit in the best way possible, considering the limits of our time, money and physical ability. By doing so, I also tried to acknowledge the impact that Aldo Leopold, author of *A Sand County Almanac* and of essays expressing the new American land ethic, had on modern life.

High above the "Swimming Hole," a well-oxygenated trout pool formed by a narrow waterfall, we saw numerous white-throated swifts flying near their nesting sites in zigzag patterns. Leighanne suggested that these rapid fliers at the canyon walls were mocking my attempts to identify bird notes and to link them with their species of origin. I refuted the possibility, saying the swifts couldn't care less about slow-walking hominids of the canyon. These swifts were reputed to be the fastest birds in North America, attaining speeds of close to 200 miles per hour. Whatever issues a flying swift might have with tourists, the bird passed them by so quickly as to be non-existent.

In thinking about the Gila country, I recalled the Native American novelist N. Scott Momaday, whose work I enjoyed reading many years ago. Momaday had said, "Once in his life a man ought to give himself up to a particular landscape in his experience; to look at it from as many angles as he can, to wonder upon it; to dwell upon it."

The Gila wasn't my "remembered earth." The country was new to me and I was getting introduced. It was all immediacy and presence, but there was something personal and familiar with the way that birds winged across my life in this locale, with the way that trout swam from the canyon waters into my blood, because I had sought them as of old. I met them in the wild, and for that the Gila wouldn't be forgotten. Still, our time here was short; I tried to concentrate intently on the place, and looked to see it from as many angles as I could.

Strolling near the cabin on a national forest road I trained binoculars on a red bird, a tanager. Again it was the summer tanager. I was hoping to find the similar hepatic tanager, with its darker cheek and bill, a species that would be a life-bird for me. Waiting on birds, I met a cowboy on a horse.

The young horseback rider paused for me as our trails converged. The fellow pushed a cowboy hat from his brow, spat tobacco juice from his mouth, and explained that he was a rancher just riding over the mountain. He spoke softly and slowly and directed as many words to his chestnut mare as he did to me. A sheathed rifle was slung to his saddle. He had been a rancher and a truck driver living near Artesia, but trying to make amends with his separated wife, he relocated to the Glenwood area. He seemed to approximate my stereotype of the Western cowboy in almost every way but one—his leisure time.

He told me he'd been riding over backcountry trails today, not exactly hunting or herding cattle, but simply trekking through the Gila out behind the Whitewater, higher up than anywhere I could go in my limited time. Referring to the canyon lands well above the Catwalk Trail, he described what he had seen: "The country is real pretty."

Thus I longed to know more. What about those canyons and those mesas he had seen or crossed? All I saw was vastness, vague and undefined. Roughly speaking, the Gila is a wilderness block about 100 miles north and south by 60 miles east and west in one of the remotest regions of the continental United States. There was no way I could know it well in a life-time, let alone in four short days. So I begged apology to the frailty of the human condition, and thanked the modern cowboy for his words.

A short time after, while drinking Mexican beer at our cabin porch, I spotted life-birds number three and four, the band-tailed dove and the gray-breasted jay. They were right in front of me in the shrubbery by the driveway. Like the big green lizard that ran across the stones to perch on a standing log, the birds were emissaries of the Gila, and together they served the country to the visitor like a waiter serving a plate.

The next morning, following the latest life-bird sighting (a Cassin's sparrow), we got another early start on the Catwalk. Where I'd previously seen a sizeable trout beneath a log in a small pool near the picnic area, I made a single cast and caught a 10-inch rainbow. In a second pool beneath a water chute upstream, I caught another trout with a singular bow cast. Okay, I thought, so where's the challenge? It would come soon enough.

At one point, boulders in the creek bed braided the flow and helped create a series of enchanting pools. I descended to a couple of the pools and started casting from my knees. The colorful hybrids rose fearlessly to the artificial, and again I quit after releasing my fifteenth or sixteenth trout of the day. With that, Leighanne and I hiked on. It was the onset of a holiday weekend and the increase in the number of trail walkers was becoming painfully obvious.

I stopped to pull half a dozen discarded water bottles from the creek, and once again cursed the mindset of those who were callous to the beauty of the land. As if to reward my good deed for the day, we were visited briefly by life-bird number six: a painted redstart that had perched in a short tree just a few feet off the trail. The bird was unmistakable with its patented red breast and black head. I saw white patches on the wings and tail. I had read that this "uncommon summer resident" of the Gila Canyonlands could be found near oak trees at an elevation between 5000 and 8000 feet. I'd been ready for this colorful creature, but discovering it was special nonetheless.

North of Glenwood is a place called Alma, population 10. We turned right at the Alma junction and proceeded eastward on a dusty corrugated road past broken trailer homes and ranches, stopping six miles later where the road dead-ended at a wooden corral. That's where Cooney Canyon opened to the valley. Cooney was named for an early gold seeker who was buried nearby. It is the lesser twin of Whitewater Canyon, if by "lesser" we mean that it's slightly smaller, maybe wilder and less visited by tourists. Like the Whitewater, Cooney is a slot canyon formed by water in the Mogollons, although today its formative agent, Mineral Creek, was dry and gone—at least in its lower end.

Standing in the lower canyon, we were probably the only humans for miles around. We were like the lost spirit of Mineral Creek except for the assurance that water could be found higher in the canyon if we ventured far enough. We listened to thunder cracking and rumbling from the peaks above, and rain was starting to patter on rocks and dust.

I had read that Mineral Creek was a place to visit if you wanted "peace, quiet, and a chance to fish for small trout." But again our timing was less than ideal. The rock columns in the canyon were spectacular, their sculpture forming a "pink box canyon." But the knife-blade edges and rectangular formations had an alien feel about them as I linked the stone and washed-out trail to the possibility of a flash flood from the storms beyond.

It was possible to climb into the canyon for a couple of miles and find a concrete remnant of the gold-mining town called Cooney. The allure was palpable but, for me at least, the desert rain made the jumbled stream bed seem foreboding. This was Billy the Kid and Butch Cassidy terrain, the place where Cooney's scalp met the Apache blade, and I was wimping out, according to my wife who's usually right about these matters. Blame it on the rain or blame it on my cowardice, my quiet walk behind Leighanne through Cooney Canyon was a futile attempt to "think like a mountain" as Aldo Leopold might do.

We found a secluded canyon seep, a mossy dooryard to a spring suggesting that water wasn't far away. But when would Mineral Creek appear? There were miles of canyon to ascend, with a couple of side trails dropping into the higher reaches from the small road above Mogollon village, but we would never see them.

We had visited Mogollon earlier. The village is a regionally famous "ghost-town" high up on the Whitewater Mesa, and we'd gotten there with a winding nine-mile climb while hugging the cliffs at 20 miles per hour. Its days of hosting 14 saloons during the gold and silver-mining era are long gone and replaced now with a modest display of artisans' gallery, antique shop, museum, and café.

The dark stillness of the canyon was interrupted by occasional voices, by the rocky syllables of thunder, and by avian notes from canyon wren, black phoebe and summer tanager. We stood in obeisance to the eerie quiet or else attempted to capture or comprehend the wildness by taking a photograph. Mineral Creek, however, was beyond us in another season or upon another level, gone within the leaves of sycamore or the otherworldly forms of rock. Its trout, the black-spotted yellowish hybrids, were relegated to imagination. I would learn that the canyon had been a candidate site for Gila trout reintroduction back in 1994, but the plan by the Recovery Team had been dashed by opposition from officials here in Catron County. The way I saw it, the loss was the county's, first and foremost.

We saw a starved black horse shuffling along in search for something edible left behind by free-roaming cattle. Its black ribs were obvious as a bleached bone on the desert floor, and its ghost of a rider was the history of human penetration into the canyons of the Gila. As we passed the black horse on the Cooney Canyon Road, we noticed that the rain had stopped and the domineering sun had reappeared.

With our early morning departure from the Glenwood cabin we paused to listen to a chorus of coyotes from across the roadway. The cacophony of yips and cries reminded us of kids shouting and screaming. The coyotes, neither pleased nor sorry to see us leave the area, had their own agenda for the edge of Gila country. I wondered how far inside the wilderness their larger cousins, the Mexican gray wolves, might be found.

124

Hopefully they were doing fine despite the hardship faced through forest fires and an element of unsupportive cattle ranchers in the state. The wolves, recently reintroduced to their native southwestern habitat, deserved their rank in the food chain and their place among the elk and mule deer populations. If cattlemen, pushing their herds through public lands along the Gila's edge, grew an extra cow or two for the wolf each year, they would probably do everyone a favor.

I thought of the gray wolf as we stopped at Aldo Leopold Vista off the highway south of Glenwood. There, in the solitude of arid ground dedicated to the great twentieth-century environmentalist and writer, a jackrabbit hopped into shade of a pinyon pine, and a family of Gambel's quail scurried for cover. A low plaque in front of us identified the mountains and canyons to the east. We saw an interface of desert and mountain worlds, an edge to our visual realm and the point from which imagination was required to make contact with the vastness of the Gila. The view we had was excellent by virtue of the land just being there for its own sake, and secondarily for whatever non-destructive pleasures that people could derive from it. This was wilderness protected by law, the country's first designated wild place, thanks to the early efforts of Aldo Leopold, a forest supervisor for the Gila. The youthful Leopold was less than fond of wolves.

Leopold shared a belief common to his time. The big predators in the southwestern food chain, the mountain lion and the wolf, were detrimental to the populations of deer and elk that sportsmen liked to hunt. As a hunter himself, Leopold freely targeted what the ranchers and hunters wanted removed. One day, after shooting into a pack of wolves with cubs, he caught up with several wounded animals. In the eyes of a dying she-wolf he observed the slow ebb of a "fierce green fire" that would later symbolize for him the glory of wild nature. The banked green fire in the gray wolf's eyes would mark him deeply in the years to come. It would change not only Leopold's opinion about the role of wolves and predators; it also revolutionized his view of nature and the balance of life.

Leopold's evolving career as a conservationist, educator, and author led him into studies far and wide. The "land ethic" that he helped formulate was one he lived by and promoted intensely. His impact on our culture is incalculable. I felt his guidance strongly when I settled in an old farmhouse many years ago.

At Silver City we climbed a small road north into the ponderosa forest. Two hours, or 45 miles later, we arrived at Gila Cliff Dwellings National Monument. The road had been a jeep trail until recent decades but the land on every side remained remote and wild. Life-bird number seven flew across my view as we proceeded. A red-faced warbler suggested that identification is easy at times—if you've planned for the possibilities to be found in each new setting. A good field guide is essential.

Fire had razed the forest only weeks ago. The so-called Miller Fire had burned through a hundred thousand acres of national forest, its blaze apparently caused by human carelessness. Even near the Visitors' Center we could smell the charred remains. But what surprised us was the green growth already pushing outward into the sun, the leaves and stems energizing from blackened stumps and roots. It was the fierce green fire of the Gila—the wildness banked and endlessly reborn.

The scene was like the "Mesa of the Angels" known to Leopold. This was dry Apache land, angular and sharp. The Gila River edges were threaded with cottonwood, sycamore and willow. Meadows were spangled with penstemon, and the canyon seeps with columbine. Here I found the deep enchantment. We had dropped down from the ponderosa pine. The high desert had eased us through the pinyon and juniper. And here the Gila with its three-pronged origins flowed beyond our comprehension. We could try to reach for an understanding of the watershed, but it was more important to relax and wallow in the moment.

We were greeted by park volunteers and then strolled upward through the leafy Cliff Dwellers' Canyon. When the trail turned sharply from a stream it followed, we got our first view – deep caves along the south-facing slope. The series of side-by-side caves reflected quiet voices of a group of visitors, words echoing perfectly in natural acoustics of the place. In the first cave I imagined a tribal sound of beating drums, of ceremonial rhythms in thirteenth-century Mogollon life, of human habitation in multi-structured caves.

We climbed stairs and ladders, learning of pre-Mogollon peoples here, and of those who would come later—the Apaches, followed by nineteenth-century white explorers, many of whom pilfered and destroyed the vestiges. A sympathetic tourist could marvel at the prospect of a home range set inside a beautiful canyon, at the certain harshness that primitive life must have known here. Settlements were of short duration, less than a lifetime in some cases. They were at the mercies of climate and human enemies despite the ideal remoteness. Today the dwellings shone in late-morning sun but also sheltered their own dark mysteries. In the canyon below the caves we could see the streaked remains of the recent Miller Fire. Since half of the circuit trail to the dwellings had been closed because of the fire, we descended by the same route we had climbed. It was an odd thing: the home range of the cave dwellers seemed worlds away from where we lived today, and yet it felt close enough beneath our skins that we could almost touch it.

Aldo Leopold eventually moved to Wisconsin to work and live, espousing the virtues of self-reliance and independence. He bought an old farm whose refurbished "shack" became the center for his inspirations. There he witnessed his place as a microcosm for earth, a living entity "vastly less alive than ourselves in degree, but vastly greater than ourselves in time and space." His book *A Sand County Almanac and Sketches Here and There* was published posthumously in 1948 and would soon be recognized as an environmental classic. The book's portrayal of a personal "home range" would inspire thousands of back-to-the-land enthusiasts (including myself) in the decades to come. The Leopold ideals of beauty, tolerance and respect were adopted slowly by many people of the later twentieth-century.

   The Leopold life was one of courage and conviction. He evolved from being an effective and utilitarian manager of southwestern forests and wildlife into a crusader for the scientific preservation of American wilderness. The land ethic he developed and promoted is a reverence to the principles of ecology. As a conservationist and educator, Leopold adhered to the belief that land comprises a community of interacting lives. It is not a singular commodity designed merely for man's consumption or manipulation. According to Leopold, to discover what makes land healthy and stable, all we have to do is roam across our rural districts with our senses on alert. We'd do well to explore our watersheds and forestlands, our home place, and to study neglected species in all seasons. We should stay in touch with wilderness and listen to the howl and cry of predator and prey.

Every part of the land is good, said Leopold, whether we understand what we see or not. We're an element of the land; our job as citizens is to learn about the natural world we live in and to act accordingly—to respect the green fire burning gently through each life.

Leighanne wanted a quick inspection of the Visitors' Center. We were scheduled to return to Alamogordo later in the day; our time was running short. Leighanne dropped me off at the trailhead close to the Middle Fork Gila River and the Visitors' Center. She would join me later.

My first choice for fishing was the West Fork Gila, flowing near the Cliff Dwellings, but its water was low because of the drought. The Middle Fork looked tempting—if I could find water cold enough for trout. The upstream hike was hot beneath a midday sun.

I crossed the river in my shorts and sandals, and the water felt tepid. In the shade of a rare cottonwood tree I rigged the three-piece fly rod and then proceeded for half a mile. The canyon walls echoed with birdsong even at this late hour. I heard orioles, thrashers and wrens. High on the west cliff was a cave that looked inaccessible. I wondered if it was the cave where explorers had found a mummified child and later donated the discovery to the Smithsonian Institute. But this was no time for distractions. Given the time constraints I had to focus on the river.

A small stone-lined spring entered from the east. I thought it might be a shot of cold water to enliven my prospects for trout. I stuck my hand into the flow and pulled it back in record time. Cold water? No, scalding water! I was surprised it wasn't boiling.

Upstream of the hot stuff the river felt icy by comparison. A large fish rolled at the surface near a bank. It may have been a carp. Beyond it was a deep, calm pool, and I laid a dry fly on its surface. A fish struck, and I missed it. Then another struck at the imitation, but the hook-up was a short one. The missed opportunity repeated itself several times and I knew that something was awry. The river's green zone had become rather lush; the hiking trail was indistinct. Maybe it was time to meet Leighanne back at the cottonwood.

The renowned fly-fisher Arnold Gingrich once wrote, "A trout is a moment of beauty known only to those who seek it." In my search for a Middle Fork trout I knew some moments of beauty *before* a fish was found. I was skunked by the Gila but my effort at fishing got rewarded with something other than trout. I saw that the link between an old streamwalker and the wilderness was strong. If I could speak of it simply, I would say that the connection was fun to wade through. I might also think of it as an "Aldo Leopold thing."

Coming Off Montana

A lot of eastern anglers have dreamed of spending time in Montana and enjoying the state's superlative fly-fishing opportunities. I am no different in that regard. After fishing the Gallatin River in 2001, I decided to return someday when I had more time for the state, especially for its mountainous southwestern sector. Nine years later I finally got the chance. I had the month of July for fishing, but unfortunately no one else I knew could join me then, so I went alone, at the sprightly old age of 60. All that winter and spring before the trip I worked to stay in physical shape by hiking on the hill behind my home, and other than a February fall on the ice and snow that broke my wrist in several places, I did fine. With the purchase of a new tent, some food for the camp-outs, and a new pair of cleated wading shoes, I was ready for Montana's streams and rivers. The motto for this trip was "Do it while you can," so I did it while I could.

On the long drive west, I paused near Sheridan, Wyoming and allowed the snow-covered mountaintops to ratchet my excitement a notch or two. On the rolling edge of the short grass hills, I watched prairie dogs posted near their den sites while a pronghorn grazed nearby. Close to the border with Montana, I passed the silhouette of an upland sandpiper on a fence post, an infrequent sighting that always delights me. I reminded myself that the journey was as much for the purpose of birding and exploration as it was to fish.

As I passed burnt foothills rising to the Absarokas in the south, I crossed the Yellowstone River while listening to Arcade Fire's album called "Funeral." I absorbed as much of birdlife as I could while driving on an interstate—bald eagle, Swainson's hawk, and magpie—where the dream-like mountains of the Yellowstone Valley rose above. This was no Lewis and Clark Expedition, certainly, but reminders of that fascinating, break-through journey were everywhere I looked.

During the evening of my third day out, I pitched the tent for the first time. I was on Georgetown Lake in the Beaverhead-Deerlodge National Forest, a semi-wild body renowned for large brook trout, though the only fish I would catch there was an ordinary rainbow. Pulling up camp next morning, I was fortunate to see the flight of a large gray bird along the ground, a bird I was able to identify with help from the knowledgeable camp host, Robert. The great gray owl, nesting in these lodgepole woods, was a life bird for me.

Rock Creek was a destination I had been anticipating for a long while. It was a "blue ribbon" trout stream even by Montana standards. I found a Forest Service camp site near its headwaters about five miles below Gillies Bridge. A one-lane, dusty, corrugated roadway followed Rock Creek for more than 50 miles downstream to its confluence with the Clark's Fork of the Snake River near Missoula. It's not a roadway anyone travels just for pleasure. Though many anglers from Missoula do ascend the Rock Creek Road, I was lucky to have solitude because the road was closed for repairs between my campground and the city. Stream conditions had improved recently following the annual run-off of the snows. I found cold clear waters rather than a muddy, turbulent flow. Whereas tourists, mosquitoes and biting ants were bothersome in camp, trout were rising to Blue-winged Olives and to stonefly patterns on Rock—albeit between pelting thunderstorms throughout this first afternoon on the creek. And things got better.

Mornings I would fish on excellent dry fly water, 50 feet wide or more, flowing fully over rock and gravel. West slope cutthroats up to 14 inches took the fly, as well as cut-bow hybrids and occasional brown trout. I had one accident: a fly hook was fired from the lip of a pissed-off bruiser and got snagged in the webbing of my cherished landing net. I tried to extricate the fly with a pair of miniature scissors but then resorted to a knife. The knife, in turn, nicked a middle finger deeply. I washed and squeezed the wound then trudged back to the car for the emergency kit. You can't have a flawless time while probing paradise, but you should stay vigilant, or risk an early termination.

I wanted to fish the feeder creek flowing past the camp site, so I grabbed a small cane rod and a four-weight line. Sure enough, cutthroat trout began to rise for a Stimulator laid down on the surface of this rushing stream. I expected fingerlings or stunted fish, not the big ones averaging nearly a foot in length. These cutthroats, possibly remaining from the spawning season earlier in spring, were far more colorful than their noted Rock Creek brethren down below the camp.

This stream that averaged maybe 10 feet wide, along with its plentiful fishery, reminded me of the Pecos River headwaters in New Mexico a couple of years before. It was that sublime. It was *that* challenging and wild, although this stream had a quiet gravel road nearby.

The tributary had its share of log jams and inviting holds for trout as it poured off the mountain slopes through spruce and fir and aspen forest. I returned to it for a second day of fishing, after hitting up Rock Creek in several more locations.

The wind was horrible on Rock, so I looked forward to bushwhacking the feeder stream above camp. I caught the first 10-inch cutthroat just a stone's throw from my tent, then headed upstream casting a Yellow Sally. I plied the pocket water, undercuts, and quiet spots behind gray boulders. I hooked, in addition to foot-long cutthroats, a massive brown trout in a piece of fast water locked between boulders and a fallen tree. The little cane rod took a deep bend as I held the downstream trout at the bank and then approached it. Unfortunately I didn't have my net along. The trout looked to be 18 inches long, but the fly popped out.

Later, as I climbed to the roadway through this splendid valley, I looked to where the creek flowed out of wooded slopes and scattered meadows. The sun was setting and reflected a golden glow and fresh tranquility from the great escarpments of rock and talus. Everything was trout-colored and new, and I gave thanks to the 14 cutthroats and five wild browns that I captured and released this day. With a final glimpse at the upper valley, I imagined swimming toward the source like a trout on a mission. Given the restraints of time and muscle, I could never walk there on my own.

All of a sudden I had fins and I could swim. It might have been a dream, but it *was* Montana.

The drive to the Bitterroot River south of Missoula was a long affair. I called my wife and daughter on the cell phone and wished the younger one a happy 21st birthday. I also wished they could be here for the fun of it, and not (nice guy that I am) for the miserable moments like the drive through the Bitterroot's heat and dust where Route 93 was getting reconstructed. I was glad to move beyond the face-lift and, miles above the last village, to settle near the headwaters on the West Fork Bitterroot. At this new camp I'd be tenting under ponderosa pines where the mountain waters sang an endless song.

First I had to pay my camp fee and do a little business with the host. I backed out my vehicle through a tight spot in the trees and heard a sickening thud as my tail light and bumper met resistance from an evergreen. Luckily my light survived the crush of plastic and metal, and the minor accident would prove to be the worst one of the trip, something even the traffic of Chicago's rush hour couldn't surpass.

That evening, as the hermit thrushes trilled along the West Fork, I engaged the spinner fall of mayflies and caught eleven trout, all of them pretty small. The big ones waited for tomorrow.

Next morning, the most interesting catch wasn't a big trout. I had a fish bobbing in my hand, escaping before my positive identification. It looked like a nine-inch brook trout, but darker and of unfamiliar proportions. I'm pretty sure it was a bull trout which, like the eastern brook, is actually a species of char. Bull trout are fairly common natives in the coldest and

135

cleanest waters of the Bitterroot tributaries. It was my first encounter with this species and, unfortunately, I wouldn't catch another.

Hours later, though, in the canyon waters below the Painted Rocks Reservoir where the Fork averages 60 feet in width, some large trout were rising to one of the most significant stonefly hatches I have ever seen. The afternoon air above the river swarmed with flies. They were back-lit by the sun and framed against a shadowed mountain. Cutthroats rose to a Golden Stonefly imitation on the surface and battled vigorously. They rose from along the nearest bank as well as from the middle of the Fork. When the stones settled down, mayfly spinners laid their eggs, and the trout took them as well. Several of the cutthroats, colorful and hefty, measured 17 and 18-inches long. I finished the day with 18 splendid trout. On the following day, however, I got a different result. That's right. The weather seemed no different then, but there was no discernible hatch, and no frenetic trout activity on the river's surface. I worked hard for the 10 fish captured and released that day.

During the night I woke to hear the crying of a western screech owl from somewhere out among the pines. This owl, like the great gray at Georgetown Lake, was a life bird for me. In the morning, while packing up to leave, I heard yet another new species in the patchy-barked trees. It proved to be the soft twittering of pygmy nuthatches, a species sounding more like the brown-headed variety of the South than the red-breasted nuthatch of the East. The pygmy loves the towering ponderosas, also known as yellow pine, a dominant tree of the West Fork. I never saw this little bird but I could hear it—after learning its notes with help from a field guide.

I got assistance of a different sort from a group of fly fishermen camped nearby. These three fellows were from Oregon and had experience with some of the rivers I planned to fish. They envied my decision to fish the Big Hole River and the Madison near Yellowstone National Park. One guy insisted I accept a few of the caddis flies that he had tied. All of these men assured me that the flies (an emerger pattern) would be deadly on the Madison, especially below the renowned Three Dollar Bridge. I thanked the gents and wished them luck. With that, I prepared for a move.

I drove southward along the East Fork Bitterroot with its miles of burnt-out forestland along the slopes. I crossed the Continental Divide and made a sharp turn on the precipitous Idaho border. At the Big Hole National Battlefield I stopped for a midday rest and to pay respects to the Nez Perce Americans who had once suffered horribly at the hands of an advancing new nation and its military might.

A woman, clerking at the Trading Post in Wisdom, Montana told me, "Hell yes, you can catch grayling anywhere around here. Just stop at the bridge outside of town. You'll find 'em."

I was on the Big Hole River, considered by some experienced anglers to be one of the finest trout streams in the world. I was after Arctic grayling, a storied fish related to trout, now found mostly in Alaska and Canada and in a few streams of the Lower 48. I didn't stop until I got 10 miles or so downriver from Wisdom, at a pull-off where the sagebrush opened out for miles and reached the snow-capped mountains.

Arctic grayling. Big Hole River. This was where I wanted to be, but the wind began to mushroom so powerfully that it shut down the fishing. I could make wonderful 50-foot roll casts with the wind at my back, but they came to naught. After a couple of hours I had to leave this scenic river and its lonesome ways. I had to leave its wide, shallow water and its bank where the wind bent down the grasses and where sandpiper chicks scuttled from my footsteps in retreat. I was disappointed but could only move away and watch for better opportunities.

At Wise River I stopped at a bar and learned about camping grounds on the Wise, a major tributary of the Big Hole. There weren't any grayling there, but the trout fishing was supposed to be good. I entered the Pioneer Mountains along the picturesque Wise and found that most of the National Forest camps were full. I took the last site in the Boulder Creek Campground where the wind was fierce and the mosquitoes ravenous. I fished the treacherous Wise, and figured my decision to camp along the stream may not have been too smart. I caught a single rainbow and looked forward to the next day when I'd leave and maybe try the Big Hole once again.

Deciding to return there *was* a wise decision. I drove upriver a dozen miles and found an access area at a campground. Drift boats plied the river, and the Saturday morning sun reflected from distant peaks. I waded upstream on the Big Hole, casting a small Tan Caddis dry. My first Arctic grayling was a mere 10 inches long, but this gray salmonid with its spreading dorsal fin was special—I had never seen one before. A half hour later I caught a second specimen. Outside of Alaska, no American river is home to more of the diminished Arctic grayling, a coveted member of the trout family, than the Big Hole. I was feeling privileged to be standing in a beautiful environment within the grayling's restricted range and catching and releasing the fish.

By afternoon I was headed back to Butte where I refueled and ate before traveling toward the Madison. Driving south on Route 287 toward Yellowstone, I passed through Ennis and eventually stopped at the Madison River where I fished near Lyons Bridge. There, in the heat of late afternoon, I suited up and caught a 13-inch rainbow in the brawling river just to prove that I could do it. Then I found a wooded campground where the West Fork Madison joins the larger river and I settled in comfortably beneath the evergreens.

The owner of a little fly shop near the site warned me to keep an eye out for bears—we were close to grizzly territory—so I paid extra attention to my food storage. Little did I know that bears would figure in my field experience near Yellowstone.

Fishing the West Fork Madison that night I caught two browns, a rainbow, and a Yellowstone cutthroat – a subspecies indicating I had crossed the "divide" from where the westslope cutthroat is the native trout. As one camper in the neighborhood told me, "It's quiet here, and convenient for visiting Yellowstone." I thought about that statement and began to wonder if I, too, should just commute to the park from here and avoid the hassle of finding a place to tent at the peak of tourist season. Ultimately I decided against the 35-mile trip to the park on a repeated basis. Yellowstone is big *within* its borders, I reminded myself, bigger than some states, and to really visit the place again, I needed to be closer.

If there is any sense of community in the fly fishing world, if a plethora of anglers and a trade that caters to it can make a show of that community, I saw it there on the Madison. And it all came with an edge of wildness guaranteed to keep you alert.

I was visited by an American dipper that flew up to me near camp. One morning, as I dozed in and out of sleep, I heard the strange calling of a sandhill crane that flew overhead. A big rabbit appeared as I washed my breakfast dishes—almost like somebody's loose domestic, but its black-rimmed ears and tail suggested snowshoe hare. And bears were a constant possibility.

Fishing the Madison was an interesting proposition. The big river was nestled between the Gravelly Range on the west and the Madison Range on the east. There was too much water then for comfortable wading, but the hefty browns and rainbows often rested close to the banks. I caught some nice ones not far from Hutchins Bridge.

One chilly morning I was up making coffee as the sun broke over the Madison peaks. I was preparing to visit West Yellowstone. There I'd shop for gifts and a few personal supplies including a Yellowstone fishing license.

At Jacklyn's Fly Shop a young clerk recognized my Slate Run (PA) fishing cap and asked if I was with the other guys from the Slate Run area, a Pennsylvania trout stream near his home town. I said I wasn't, and immediately realized that Yellowstone was going to be one busy place, indeed. The clerk shrunk my world even further, telling me that his older brother was the current fly-casting champion of the planet. The champs's home town was also near Slate Run, and yes, of course, I'd heard of him.

The next day I was moving into the park and it was crowded from the get-go. I was told that every campground had been filled the day before, a Monday. I would have to find a place outside the far northeastern gateway. Driving over Mt. Washburn, the park's highest point, I stopped and walked out on a spur to scan the slopes for grizzly bear and other exotics. By the time I reached America's Serengeti (the Lamar River Valley), I was feeling the need to fly fish. It was hot at midday, and the deep green river looked inviting. The Lamar gave up an 18-inch hybrid for inspection on my first outing there. The trout was a splendid cut-bow, a combination of rainbow and Yellowstone cutthroat, which had risen from behind a boulder to take a Stimulator on the surface. As I climbed back up the hill to my car, sweating profusely in the sun, I almost stumbled over a bison lying in the sagebrush, switching its tail at insects and kicking at the dust with one leg.

I left the park via the rugged mountains in the northeast sector and entered the gateway village of Cooke City, Montana. I needed a place to camp. The gas prices had suddenly climbed by 51 cents per gallon, but at least the beer was cold. The first campground I came to, Soda Butte, was also full, but another Forest Service ground, a mile up the mountain, had one last spot for a tent, and there I quickly pounded stakes. The Colter camp was exposed to the wind and had no water—but campers could obtain it out of pumps at the sister ground of Soda Butte.

Pilot Mountain rises above timberline to a point 11,699 feet above sea-level. My view of it from Colter was a close one, just across the highway out of Cooke City. As I glassed the mountain with binoculars and fought off a horde of mosquitoes, I saw whitish animals near the summit. Were they goats or sheep? My neighbor, an older fellow named Gene, grabbed a spotting scope from his RV and we saw them clearly—Rocky Mountain sheep, with brown rumps, males with sweeping horns, and ewes with their young, about 14 or 15 total, grazing in the evening sunlight on the grasses of a copper-colored slope.

Another camper rushed up to Gene's place as we watched the sheep. Did we want to see a cow moose with her calf? Sure. Where were they? Close by, but not yet in sight. And then we saw the moose emerging from some trees beside my tent, a huge mama and her calf striding slowly by us on the driveway next to Gene's RV. I was closer to wild moose than I ever wanted to be, and I hoped then and there a big wild animal never tangled with the ropes that helped support my tent against the wind.

That night it had to happen. I wasn't about to see my grizzly bear yet, but the sounds that awoke me in the tent at 1:30 certainly had me thinking in that line. The grunts and growling noises came with a menace that was mitigated slightly by a more soothing crush of grasses and shrubs. The growls had a depth to them as they resonated in my clearing situated at about 8,500 feet in altitude. I turned on my lantern, stepped outside and then turned off the light. There was no way to scare off buffalo. They have an agenda that is resolute. They graze, they mate, they can meet you face to face, whether on the highway or the trout stream, and you move aside for them. I had fished next to resting bison on a number of occasions and had never known them to make such an ugly sound, but I had never been with them after dark, at least at this close range. I didn't want them tripping over my tent with me inside. A half-ton of wild buffalo in the dark is too much for anyone to bear... and have I mentioned bears already?

During my second night at this campground the bison came again. The night before, there had been at least 10 of them passing through the grounds, according to an eye-witness report. One consolation had been the view of the Milky Way overhead. Gene had told me to observe it if I stepped outside to pee. I'd be surprised at how absolutely clear the sky would seem. And I *was* surprised, despite the presence of invisible bison. Standing at a high mountain elevation, the Milky Way seemed to envelope me in a rush like vertigo, scattering my atoms far and wide until I fell back to the relative safety of the tent. My second night there, sleep had been interrupted by a series of thundershowers. By the time the buffalo reappeared, I'd had enough. I scrambled toward the car, ears filled with their grunting and huffing sounds. Before I got through the tent door, I popped a lens from my eyeglasses that I'd foolishly set in the way. It was 4 o'clock and I got no comfort from the stars. I slept in the car till dawn.

I fished inside the park for several days, casting on Soda Butte and Slough creeks and on the Yellowstone River, but the best fishing then was on the Lamar, about 20 miles from camp. A favorite spot was on a big bend of the river, well away from the road, and partly shaded by cottonwoods and willow trees. A couple of pronghorns rested close behind me, as well as a solitary bison. A brief caddis hatch brought the trout slashing at the surface, and I caught several of the Yellowstone cutthroats, darkly spotted and buttery-toned, that taped out close to 17 inches.

I had to leave when an aggressive bull approached the resting buffalo, forcing it to move, and then headed straight for me, good-for-nothing that I was. The big guy entered the river, swam across, and then slowly clambered up the opposite bank. It was just as well because a powerful wind had been gathering force and driving the buffalo dust, driving it imperially across the valley and shutting down the fishing attempts, at least in this location. I would learn that it was the same wind that hit gusts of 70 mph in another location—my campground, where it ripped out a corner ring on my tent and partly collapsed my temporary home. It was part of the weather system that unfortunately victimized a group of young mountain climbers in the neighboring Tetons, separating one man from his support system and dropping him 2000 feet to his death.

I was looking for bear and wolf; I was hitting long traffic jams created by the bison herds near Cooke City. One night at Colter, a camper related his most recent park experience. He and his wife had stopped to watch a grizzly bear that was feeding on a dead elk. Behind the bear were several wolves that waited patiently along Soda Butte Creek for a chance to eat when the bear had had its fill. What struck the observer as most unusual was the presence of fishermen near the bear. Apparently the anglers kept their focus on the stream as if nothing else mattered. I related, sort of, but I'm pretty sure I would've backed off from the scene, to watch it near a gathering human crowd that finally moved away on the advice of a passing ranger.

The night before I left my camp across from Pilot Mountain, I was wakened again, but not from growling buffalo. A loud vehicle was zooming up the lonely highway out of Cooke City and climbing the mountain near my tent. No doubt the casino and bars of Cooke had just closed for the night. The vehicle came to a screeching, tire-burning halt. It started up again and roared ever closer. And it came to yet another screeching halt, the engine off. A female exited and laughed so loudly at her male companion that it sounded like she was in the campground itself. My friends the buffalo were roaming the highway like cops in Chicago. I imagined that Pilot Mountain, looming overhead as it had for centuries while guiding warriors and trappers and frontiersmen, got a mountain's chuckle out of one more set of people in a hurry.

I made my last departure from this campground on the edges of the Absaroka-Beartooth Wilderness on a Friday morning. I would make it home the following Tuesday, the same evening when the Soda Butte Campground (the place, a mile from my tent, where I'd loaded up on water for my washing details) suffered an event that would make the national news. Bidding adieu to the mountains surrounding Cooke City, I stopped at an information display beyond the village and learned that the burnt lands I'd been viewing on the slopes were charred in the Yellowstone fires of 1988. It was then that Cooke City almost lived up to its name, stopping the fires within a few feet of the business district.

Passing through the national park a final time, I saw my grizzly bear in a meadow between the roadway and the Lamar. The bruin was rooting leisurely in a prairie dog town. I watched it for half an hour that morning, an adult carnivore, dark with lighter patches

145

of hair at the shoulder, dining on the soil and whatever contents it contained.

Driving home at a leisurely pace along Route 20 in Wyoming, I was still fueled by the Yellowstone experience and my observations of the bear, so I pulled off the highway when I came to a place called Duck Swamp Environmental Area. This nature reserve was located in a large oxbow of the Bighorn River. There I walked a desert bluff overlooking the swamp, enjoying an opportunity to extend the sense of wildness I had gained in the West. I read interpretive signs placed along a half mile path and found the area to be an excellent transition zone, a buffer to the heavily populated eastern states. I still had wonderful locales to pass through, like the Wind River Canyon and the Sand Hills of Nebraska, but here in the warm solitude of sage and cactus I had birds: ducks and rails squawked in the marsh grass; two new life birds—the sage thrasher and the lark sparrow—flew up out of arid brush. From Duck Swamp and my eastward drive along Route 20, I could come off Montana and the Yellowstone like a butterfly to a flower.

I arrived home on a Tuesday night, the night of an incident occurring at the Soda Butte Campground near Cooke City, my springboard for the national park. I read about the tragedy the weekend after. It wasn't bison that bothered anyone, but a grizzly bear with three cubs. Several tents were torn apart during the night; a man from Michigan was killed; an unrelated woman suffered serious wounds; a young fisherman from Colorado had his journey interrupted. According to the media, everyone had properly stored away their food and other grizzly bear enticements; it was the "most brazen" (unprovoked) bear attack in the continental U.S. since the 1980s. The sow grizzly bear was trapped and, with help from DNA testing, proven to be the killer. She was euthanized. Biologists, studying her cubs (also trapped, but then transported to the zoo in Billings, Montana), determined that the young ones had been badly underfed and malnourished. I felt bad for everyone involved, bear and human. I had been there four days earlier. Sadness was a blanket I spread over the occurrence as I learned of it. The sadness even covered the fact that I was glad the wayward grizzly hadn't come for me. Like a bear in a den, I was pleased to be back home.

Springbound

Warblers

When I found the nest with eggs, I didn't know much about the hooded warbler species. I had first encountered the bird species in Virginia, but when I found the nest and, later, several males singing in our local forest, my world of warblers really opened up.

A male hooded warbler erupted with a ringing volley of notes. Its mate flew anxiously around a brushy clearing left by lumbering activities a couple summers previous. "Common in moist deciduous woods with abundant undergrowth," said my trustworthy field guide, but the warbler wasn't so common in my New York foothills that I could expect it without a bit of searching.

Tail feathers of the female hooded warbler spread out like those of a redstart, revealing flashy spots of white. I retreated from the tangled plants and brambles then, watching, realized I must have nearly trampled an unseen nest. The male's resounding and melodious *te-wee te-wee te-o* notes formed a rapid song with a slurred ending. Then his bright yellow face peered from under a black hood stretching down to the neck and chest. His underside was solid yellow; his wings and back were a dingy olive. I retreated farther, but would find the nest in a day or two.

Before I left the woods I saw a dark-eyed junco disappear between a stump and a cluster of fern. This small bird's nest was bedded under a tussock of grass. It contained four day-old nestlings opening their mouths in unison as I briefly uncovered the world above them. It was in the same clearing where I'd find the warbler's nest, the latter woven into stems of a blue cohosh plant.

The warbler's nest was only 16 inches off the ground. It was built out of leaves and grasses and contained four eggs, only one of which the warbler laid. The eggs of hooded warblers are white, with a wreath of lilac spots around the wider end. The three other eggs in the nest, uniformly blotched with chestnut configurations, had been laid there by a brown-headed cowbird, North America's notorious parasitic species.

Figuring that the hooded warbler had enough problems with regard to survival (like many songbirds that winter in the vanishing forests of our tropical regions), I decided to remove the cowbird eggs from the nest. If hatched, the young would easily outgrow and out-compete the warbler nestling. Removal was a risk because the female warbler might abandon the nest soon afterward, but that was preferable to having her raise more cowbird young. Pulling off the robbery, I cursed all cowbirds, an invasive species not unlike the lumbermen raising havoc in summer woods, encouraging a black bird that thrives in open and disturbed habitats.

Eventually I found that the junco nest had been uprooted and destroyed, most likely by a skunk. The nest's location had been just a few feet off an old lumber trail, a grassy route for various predators. It too had been victimized by forest fragmentation. Hoping to find more signs of hooded warblers, I edged farther into the woods as dusk approached. The hill was far from somnolent. Canada warblers, nesting in a hemlock jumble, sang their shrill territorial notes, and several flying squirrels flashed white bellies, skin taut, as they leapt from tree to tree.

The warbler forest near my home was at least two miles long and half a mile wide, but some of it had been logged in recent years, and sections had been damaged by an ice storm. Near an area chaotic with fallen logs and branches, now recovering with a flush of vegetation, I heard what I thought were call notes of a hooded warbler. Upon closer inspection I found that the notes actually belonged to a mourning warbler. The burst of notes from ground level mocked my ignorance as I stood there about 12 feet from the singer. I could see the slate-blue head as it alternately chided my appearance and stabbed at irksome mites.

As I made a list of birds near the logging roads I also found myself naming the trails I walked upon. A path near the defunct junco and warbler nests became "Cowbird Lane." A trail near a former heron rookery (where I'd found that so-called turkey hunters had slaughtered the squawking young in several heron nests) became "Old Heron Path." A trail tangent to a clearing with a bathtub in it (formerly used as a watering hole for cows) became "Tub Street." A path where I'd spooked a flock of turkeys was "Turkey Trail" (appropriately enough), and "Dead Beech Boulevard" was named for its litter of fallen trees. Sure,

I may have been acting on a childhood impulse or an immature fascination, but I was gaining familiarity with the hillside acreage and its lives. My rationale for naming these specific locales was that I could now impress the landform in my consciousness. I could help myself in better understanding the wild.

I sat on a stump one morning where Old Heron Path converged with Tub Street. The sun rose through the haze above the valley. I listened to birds—perhaps upwards of 30 species, even bluebirds—intermittently chiming, drumming, piping, warbling, trilling, cawing, whistling, and exhorting. I thought, so *this* is what it's like to live in poetry, to live beyond the point where one creates or reads a poem with words... I may have been reeling in a world of mental brambles, but it seemed like holding a mirror to the living points of inspiration. This was cut terrain, unusually rugged for this section of New York, where a deep ravine opened near a summit, where signs from an ice storm and from earlier lumbering activities, plus the rediscovered realm of warblers, brought me to attention.

If these bird events had a grand finale, it came where Dead Beech veered sharply downhill. First, I saw a male hooded warbler, with a white moth in its bill, drop down to a nest in the heavy undergrowth. A group of juncos suddenly buzzed and chirped like young kids who were caught with their hands in cookie jars. A family of five winter wrens, perhaps inspired by the juncos, started chattering anxiously from the undergrowth as I approached to peer inside. Yellow-bellied sapsuckers yakked from a dead tree overhead. And more birds came to the call.

A black-throated blue warbler (seldom seen in this terrain) flew in to the convocation, and it seemed that the thicket boiled with avian excitement. I couldn't have felt more involved had I stood beneath a nineteenth-century flight of passenger pigeons. I slipped away for several minutes to review what was going on, and then returned, wondering if I'd get a similar reaction from the birds. I got nothing—no birds on the path or in the undergrowth, no sign but a distant woodpecker tapping out the rhythm of its hunger. I was lucky to have been a part of something different here, something mysterious, and still unfolding with possibility as I reconsidered from afar.

Fall Landlockeds

I was ready for a change of pace, and was hoping that to fish for landlocked salmon would allow me to keep in balance with the planet. As usual, there was a major crisis developing in the world, and my father, aged 87 and in the last year of his life, aptly grumbled that "everything's going to hell in a hand basket." The financial realms had struck an iceberg in the sea of money and were tipping like a new Titanic. As the media proclaimed, the mushrooming crisis was the worst of its kind since the Great Depression. Government deregulation and old-fashioned greed had really pulled a good one this time. I, too, felt the pressure though I didn't really have a lot at stake. I was only surprised that a huge economic and political collapse had taken this long to occur. Perhaps with a big salmon on the fly line I could pull myself out from the collective funk and get refocused.

So, again the world was on a hell-bound train and I was going fishing. I'd been catching Pacific salmon of the Great Lakes region every autumn for years, but a two-year quest for Finger Lake landlockeds hadn't been fulfilled. If I could catch one landlocked salmon on a fly, the broken world would get repaired— or so I fantasized.

Landlockeds are essentially Atlantic salmon that have lost their seaward instinct. They're a little smaller than their famous counterpart but, unit for unit, are no less a game fish for the angler. Living about 100 miles from where these salmon make their spawning run from Cayuga Lake through Ithaca, New York, I had only two or three shots at the fish per year. And the salmon runs depended on sufficient autumn rain to get them moving from the bigger water. Here my window of opportunity was usually small.

In my first year of fishing for them I had several landlockeds on the line, but the hard-fighting fish escaped before I could make an introduction. Having tasted the landlocked's energy and streamlined beauty, I pursued the quest for a second year but high water levels, plus the fact that I was fishing for Pacific salmon and for steelhead then, kept me from success. The third year I did better.

The landlocked is a silver-sided fish with dark spots, a denizen of cold New England waters (and of Finger Lakes where it was introduced) where glacial retreats and deposition had blocked its passage to the ocean. It is an Atlantic salmon that's become landlocked, a species content to stay in deep lakes and rivers and to spawn in suitable feeder streams. The landlocked's diet is primarily smelt, and if the fly angler skillfully applies a reasonable imitation of a smelt at the right time and place, success should come.

I looked at my pursuit as a form of therapy. I still needed that five-pound fireball of energy to set things right and to give me a renewed sense of purpose. If the new global economy was beset with a surfeit of players, all that my own economy needed was a version of Atlantic salmon that had slightly smaller eyes and shorter fins than its well-known counterpart.

The long-awaited rain arrived in late October. Then one morning, under a somber sky spitting snow, I approached my Ithaca water flowing through its gorge. Dressed in sweatshirt, poncho and neoprene waders, I was set for the elements. I spoke with an angler who'd already caught an eight-pound brown trout on an egg-skein. Landlockeds had arrived as well, and I employed a dark Wooly Bugger with a chartreuse head to stir them into action. Salmon don't feed on a spawning run, but an attractor fly or egg pattern often gets them to strike instinctively.

Searching for salmon in a creek or river is a form of sight-fishing that requires full attentiveness and a slow approach. It's like hunting then, and I found that a hunt for landlockeds is more deliberate than a search for the massive Pacific salmon farther north. I tried to stay attentive to the variations of light and water, to the depth of flow, to various sounds and motions both in the water and beyond. Sometimes I would pause for a glimpse of the beautiful waterfall upstream, one of several that Ithaca is renowned for.

A salmon clamped down on the fly, rose briefly from the water and with a twist was gone. Encouraged, I stepped backward into midstream and waited for the salmon to return. I laid out another cast just upstream of the fish, allowing the fly to swing across its view. I was surprised that the fish struck the fly a second time. After a brief battle, I raised the dark male from the creek's edge, measured it along the rod at 20 inches, noted the kype, or hooked jaw, then let the handsome fish return. The quest was won.

Through the morning I caught and released several more of its kind. One of the fish, a silvery female with a blue-green back, was smooth as marble and 22 inches long. Although I'd eventually cast with luck for landlocked salmon in Maine and northern New Hampshire, my outings closer to home were special accents highlighting the local water.

Returning to my car parked near the impressive Ithaca Falls, I saw a slogan painted on the rocks. Its message was, "Live free, or die fighting." I had no real clue about the meaning, other than in order to exist freely in this age, you had to make sense of the madness and live accordingly. I saw several signs with a clearer message: "Impeach Bush." Thankfully a new presidential election was imminent, and though an election rarely gives me a chance to renew hope, I knew that any change had to be for the better. And having wrestled with salmon through the day, I could drive home like a vessel with straight sailing.

Winter Count

Late summer, and I felt the "empty nest" syndrome. My son had just gone back to his academic work in Washington D.C., and my daughter had just flown off to France for a semester abroad. She'd be gone until Christmas. My wife and I faced a season's drapery that reflected shades of loneliness.

I forged on with the essay I was writing, the next part of which was the piece, "Winter Count." It concerned my 20 consecutive years participating as a volunteer for the Audubon Christmas Count in the fields and forests of neighboring Allegany County.

I was making new connections. When my wife and I had taken Alyssa to catch her plane for France, I saw a mourning dove fallen upright, alive, on a sidewalk by the airport terminal. A feathery smudge marked the glass wall overhead. I hoped the dove would recover. Then, home again, I found a freshly killed veery by the side of our road. The body of this species of thrush remained limp; its wash of olive-brown coloration on the back was still unruffled. No doubt what had started as a passage of migration had become yet another instance of road kill, and it started to symbolize my melancholy when I thought about time's progression.

When I looked ahead to my writing and another winter count to come, I saw diminishment. By late fall and December the great majority of birds have flown from this sector of the state. In my portion of the count area, a section of a circle with a 15-mile diameter in the rural landscapes near Scio, New York, I'm lucky to find 20 species of bird life in a half day of the annual survey. If I counted there in early summer I could probably find upwards of 75 species of birds. In winter, though, I take diminishment for granted, knowing that the time for cold weather and rest is necessary and inevitable, and a struggle, too, for those unable to hibernate or move away. To help myself and the world of science keep a tab on bird life in these changing times, I count on the designated day.

I was writing outside on a late August afternoon when I paused to look up at the swallows circling anxiously farther and farther from their old nesting sites in the barn. Within days they'd be gone, departed on migration to a southern continent. I looked back to the notes I had written following a Christmas count in the 1990s.

On 18 December 1994, I participated in the 32nd annual Christmas Bird Count in the Scio circle for the Audubon Society and the Allegany County Bird Club. It was my fourth consecutive year. I focused on the 1666 acres of Plumbottom State Forest near Amity Lake. The sky was overcast and threatening snow or rain, but I was comfortable and content. During the eight hours of my count I walked four miles and drove slowly over the 42 miles within my designated area.

I found 24 species of birds and counted individuals for each of them. It was the most I ever tallied in my 20 years of the Christmas count. Among these birds I listed were a great horned owl, a brown creeper, a pileated woodpecker, a rough-legged hawk, two ravens, two red-breasted nuthatches, 18 golden-crowned kinglets, 86 cedar waxwings, 125 black-capped chickadees, and a dozen American robins, a couple of which sustained half-hearted songs that were rather weak but pleasant to these winter ears. I felt like singing back to them, "O come all ye Druids, tis the season, almost, for the Solstice," but I didn't, deciding to trudge on quietly in this time of cold diminishment.

One winter I began a comprehensive study of reported bird sightings at Keeney Swamp in northeastern Allegany County. I began to read the newsletters issued by the Allegany County Bird Club from its start in the 1960s to a point some three decades later. Dedicated observers of bird life in this area preserved their records of sightings throughout Allegany County, and I took it upon myself to note which observations pertained to the large wetland area known as Keeney Swamp. I felt that the remote location was significant for a program being developed by the Audubon Society of New York State.

The Society wanted a guide that conservationists could use to help protect essential habitat for birds throughout New York State. A similar tool was being developed for other states as well. A regional guidebook would be published. That volume, eventually entitled *Important Bird Areas in New York State*, would list in detail 127 sites considered essential to the preservation and well-being of many different kinds of birds. Jeffrey Wells, director of New York Audubon's bird conservation and Important Bird Area (IBA) program, said, "We want to give these sites priority for land acquisition, research, and educational monies." Along with my friend Sean Phelan, from Allegany County, N.Y. (who went on to record numerous other first-hand observations in Keeney Swamp), I hoped to get enough pertinent data, based on state-specific criteria, from the 2,170-acre Keeney Swamp State Forest to have it evaluated and eventually listed in the IBA book. To have the state forestland approved and to have its conservation issues considered on a scientific basis would become one of the finest feathers I could stick in my environmental cap.

Keeney Swamp is roughly 30 percent deciduous forest, 30 percent non-tidal wetland, 20 percent coniferous forest, and 20 percent shrub and grassland. It's used as a conservation-natural area, with some recreational and forestry use, along with water supply. Current threats to the land come from recreational overuse, succession of critical habitat, and cowbird parasitism. The land includes a "Sub-Canadian Zone" with native stands of balsam fir. And, as the IBA book states it, "A major strength of this site is its diversity of birds and other wildlife."

Sean Phelan was coordinator of the New York State Atlas 2000 bird count in the area of Keeney Swamp, a five-year project. He observed that 114 species of birds were nesting in its confines. Many other species were noted, as well, but were considered migratory since observations were either prior to or following the known breeding dates for them. Some years before the 2000 Atlas count, I walked through the Keeney forestland on a beautiful day in May and counted 86 species of birds, a personal one-day record for me at the time.

During the season of winter snow and ice, I always look forward to the coming days when the sap begins to flow and the red-winged blackbirds return to Keeney Swamp, beginning the surge of bird life in its myriad forms to the uplands of New York. Surely then the blank spots on the map of the human soul begin to green once more, and birds repopulate the depths within.

The Spring

The tributary flows through the remotest section of the river's watershed. Its valley is mostly forested, with intermittent clearings where willow trees and alders predominate, and the brook's flow is mostly paralleled by a jeep trail that provides limited access to a series of small hunting camps. I've fished the brook in springtime for nearly a decade and have never seen another human on those walks.

Today the brook was low and clear. I like to fish it with a very short fly rod (5'9") and an even shorter leader on a weight-forward line. The stream banks are stable, with undercuts and overhangs, and experience with the fly rod comes in useful on this feeder stream. The brook trout here are wild, extremely wary; and even early in the season, on a late April day, the otherwise pleasurable fishing is a challenge.

About two miles from the brook's mouth in this headwaters region (where I gain my access), there's a wonderful spring that hangs on the rock and moss above one bank. That was my destination today. I consider it one of the wild sources of a major river system near my home. Although today marks the 40th anniversary of Earth Day in this country, that's entirely coincidental. I was walking more in line with the coercive draws of an attractive spring.

In the lower forest I was often pinched by downfalls and by low-hung branches where I had to use an underhand swing of the line, or else I made a careful "bow-and-arrow cast" to a likely spot for brook trout. I listened to the bright, acidic notes of the blue-headed vireo, an early migrant to these woods where the growth of wild leeks and deadly hellebore was well underway. I enjoy this micro-fishing with a fly rod, and today the beautiful native trout was flush with much of my anticipation and sense of discovery.

This back country stream averages only four or five feet in width. I worked my way up through the hollow, alone with my thoughts, toward a natural spring significant enough to be labeled "Spring" on the topographic map of this area. A winter wren, with its stub tail and eye stripe, flitted from an undercut bank to perch on a mossy log. As it broke into a long and intricate song, the stone-sized bird seemed perfect for this woodland habitat.

The native brook trout (*Salvelinus fontinalis*) is actually a char, and not a trout. The species name, *fontinalis*, translates into "the dweller of springs," and that's what counts. Many of the five-inch brook trout that I catch here and release are gorgeous, their resplendent coloration reminiscent of those larger fish that spawn here in autumn. Even in springtime there's a chance of catching brook trout of more than 10 inches, a truly big fish for a mountain stream this size.

I crept on hands and knees to a deep hole underneath a leaning hemlock tree and dropped the artificial fly inside. I quickly latched on to a 10-inch brookie and could sense the poetry of a stream experience in the river of time. I was *not* alone in this company of the wild.

A ruffed grouse exploded from the thickets where the season's first trillium and hepaticas bloomed. Hepaticas are a favorite wildflower and I didn't want to leave them behind. I entered a boggy glade where alders hold down the precious soils and there I took a simple lunch break. The season for wild turkey hunting hadn't yet begun, and there was no sign of a human footprint.

I reentered the woods, keeping in mind my upstream appointment with not only the spring but also with a deep pool formed by fallen trees. I wanted to reacquaint myself with a couple of excellent brook trout living there. On fishing the splashy pool, it was good to find my friends still living at the site.

Again the land opened up. A buried gas line crossed the valley and made it seem wider and more light-filled. The countryside was a patchwork of private lands, an unprotected domain. With the current push for gas production from Marcellus Shale that underlies this region (an industrial process that requires hydro-fracturing of the shale with millions of gallons of stream water and with sand and chemicals for each well that is built), I was worried for the land and its special, rural qualities.

I stepped to the jeep trail that runs parallel to much of the brook and studied the posted signs displayed along its edges by the various landowners, most of whom lived in distant cities, and a few of whom had granted me the privilege of fishing. A pair of woodcock flew up from a puddle on the trail and circled over the posted territories.

Inside the forest, I came to an old picnic table someone had set beside the trail. Both benches and the table-top were carpeted with lush green moss. No doubt it had been placed here so a resting soul could gaze at the spring. I, too, sat gently on a bench and looked at the spring that issued from a steep bank across the brook. Water gushed down a 45-degree slope, a sheet of cold spring water 50 feet in length and nearly 30 feet high. It rippled down through stone and grass and fell to the brook inhabited by wonderful little char.

I climbed to the edge of the spring and cupped my hands. I drank deeply, almost feeling like a poacher, even though I'd left my fly rod on the mossy table below, even though, in the strictest sense, no one was around for miles, and no one really owned the earth. It was Earth Day, and I returned to the table where I wrote a few words in a note-pad. Then glancing at the spring, I recognized I was here on an ordinary day when nothing much was happening. It was special, though, a day unlike all others.

About the Author

Walt Franklin is a writer, educator and naturalist who ventures outdoors as much as he can. He is an active member of the Slate Run Sportsmen in Pennsylvania and Trout Unlimited in New York. His collection of fly-fishing essays, *River's Edge*, is in print along with two other collections, *A Rivertop Journal* and *Sand & Sage*. He has also written and published *Uplands Haunted by the Sea*, *The Wild Trout*, and several other slender volumes of poetry. He lives in an old farmhouse near Greenwood, New York with his wife, Leighanne.

Check out his regularly posted fly-fishing blog at **www.rivertoprambles.wordpress.com**

For more information about Walt's work and similar writings, visit the Wood Thrush Books website at **www.woodthrushbooks.com**

.

Made in United States
North Haven, CT
13 October 2022

25416845R00104